CW00704107

The Dull Stone House.

Kenner Deene

The Dull Stone House, etc.
Deene, Kenner
British Library, Historical Print Editions
British Library
1862
2 vol. ; 12º.
12624.b.7.

The BiblioLife Network

This project was made possible in part by the BiblioLife Network (BLN), a project aimed at addressing some of the huge challenges facing book preservationists around the world. The BLN includes libraries, library networks, archives, subject matter experts, online communities and library service providers. We believe every book ever published should be available as a high-quality print reproduction; printed on- demand anywhere in the world. This insures the ongoing accessibility of the content and helps generate sustainable revenue for the libraries and organizations that work to preserve these important materials.

The following book is in the "public domain" and represents an authentic reproduction of the text as printed by the original publisher. While we have attempted to accurately maintain the integrity of the original work, there are sometimes problems with the original book or micro-film from which the books were digitized. This can result in minor errors in reproduction. Possible imperfections include missing and blurred pages, poor pictures, markings and other reproduction issues beyond our control. Because this work is culturally important, we have made it available as part of our commitment to protecting, preserving, and promoting the world's literature.

GUIDE TO FOLD-OUTS, MAPS and OVERSIZED IMAGES

In an online database, page images do not need to conform to the size restrictions found in a printed book. When converting these images back into a printed bound book, the page sizes are standardized in ways that maintain the detail of the original. For large images, such as fold-out maps, the original page image is split into two or more pages.

Guidelines used to determine the split of oversize pages:

• Some images are split vertically; large images require vertical and horizontal splits.
• For horizontal splits, the content is split left to right.
• For vertical splits, the content is split from top to bottom.
• For both vertical and horizontal splits, the image is processed from top left to bottom right.

12624 б.7.

THE

DULL STONE HOUSE.

KENNER DEENE.

IN TWO VOLUMES.

VOL II.

T. CAUTLEY NEWBY, PUBLISHER.
30, WELBECK STREET, CAVENDISH SQ.
1862.

THE

DULL STONE HOUSE.

CHAPTER I.

AN ANGEL'S FACE.

WHAT a title for the heading of a chapter!
Absurd!! Yes, to those who believe that
angel's faces never shine upon us here
on earth; that they are never round our
paths, nor about our beds. That their voices
never fall on our ears, making sweet echo-
ing music, which shall reverberate long,
long after other worldly sounds have ceased
to interest us, have ceased to echo at all.
But the face of one of these gentle ones
was to beam on Paul Withers's pathway. It

was not the face of Margaret Percy. No. That was a beautiful face enough. Like a sculptured marble in repose; like what it was, a lovely woman's face when animated, but never an angel's face.

Paul did not even think so for one moment, in all the wild and hopeless love he lavished on Miss Percy. Her attributes were very earthly. She was beautiful; she was even gentle. She looked earnestly, truthful, and tender, sometimes through those violet eyes of hers. If that was her soul looking through the eyes, it *was* not a sordid or a vulgar soul, but she was not an angel.

Paul loved her. He had only seen her twice; but he loved her, and was as weak and yielding to this passion as are most of us, when *first love* comes upon us in its resistless might, in all its o'ermastering strength, in its overwhelming power. He yielded himself up to this mad feeling; he counted the days that must intervene before each visit to Percy Priory, and when he entered the shade of its beech woods, he counted breathlessly his chances of seeing Margaret, of hearing her voice, of dwelling entranced on its every tone. Where is all this to end? When once passion has fairly usurped the mastery, did ever this prudent question recal one being to a sense of prudence? I trow not.

Paul went on his way, not rejoicing, scarcely fearing; treasuring up looks and smiles which *she* dealt out impartially to all. He hoped for nothing definite, only for the next time of meeting her; only for another chance, and another, of gazing upon her beauty, of hearing her speak, perhaps even of touching her hand.

She would always stop and speak to him in the street, kindly too, and with a light shining over the pure perfect face, as though his presence gave her pleasure. But Miss Percy behaved thus gently to everybody. She had very suave manners. And then, Paul had saved her life. One day, just when the first flush of autumn had

faintly flooded the woods with its glow; just
at the season when the fairy-like white
mists rise spiritually in the deep green
grass; just when the autumn fruit blushes
rosy upon the trees, and the first glory of
summer's roses is passing away; just at this
season, one golden morning, Paul Withers
rode through the lands of the Percys.

He was not going to see the heir, he was
going to see Margaret. She was ill. He
found her stretched on a sofa, in a small
boudoir, a lovely little room, quite a lady's
bower. He had never seen anything so
perfect of its kind before. It was a small
room opening into the conservatory, where
rich rare blossoms blended their hues
superbly. The drapery in this room was of
rose coloured silk. The ceiling was painted
exquisitely. The couch on which Margaret
lay, in her white morning dress, was also
rose coloured. Her face was changed. It
was even wan, and the lovely violet eyes
were somewhat sunken. The tall, stately
Cecil Percy stood by her side, and he in-

clined his head very stiffly indeed when Paul entered.

"Miss Percy is very unwell, Mr.—Mr.—"

"Withers," said Paul.

"Oh," said Mr. Percy, without repeating the name.

Paul felt the pulse. His own fluttered strangely. The girl's slight hand lay in his.

"Very feverish," said he.

Margaret sighed. Then Paul began to look for pen and paper. He wrote a pre-scription. He rose. It was time for him to go, but he lingered. He lingered un-bidden, and spoke a few words of advice.

"Air. Miss Percy should go out every day. Should walk."

"I will, Mr. Withers, when I possibly can," said Margaret. "But I feel very poorly to-day."

"Do you sleep well?" asked Paul.

Across the sculptured marble of the face there passed a vivid flush at this simple, natural question, and she turned the blue eyes away, and when she spoke, it was in a low tone.

" Not very."

Not very. It was some trouble then, some affection of the spirits that weighed down this softly-nurtured lady, and laid her fainting on her silken couch. It was some inward fever that caused the light to fade out of her eyes. Paul loved her. He would have given his life for her. She was his dream by day, his thought by night, and a fierce jealousy consumed him. She loved some one. Whom did she love? If he could only know. Not that it would do any good, but still, just to know the worst. But he knew nobody that Miss Percy knew. He was a being of a different order. Quite a creature beneath her. Nothing, in her eyes, positively nothing; and he went out from her presence, that golden autumn day, completely awakened from his dream of the two last months, awakened, but wretched, loving her still, but knowing the full extent of his misery. He had given his best love, his deepest feelings, his whole being, to a woman who would never know that he had suffered anything for her sake; and if she did know, she would either laugh him to scorn, or fire with indignation at his presumption; and he must go on loving this woman all his miserable life, with no hope before him. None. He must never try to move her pity, nor awaken her sympathy. He must suffer, and be dumb.

Cecil Percy, the younger, was coming from the dining-room with his nurse when Paul passed. He ran up to him and put his little hand in that of Paul. "I'm quite well now," he said. "I'm to go out on the pony every day, and I'm never to take physic any more, am I?"

Paul paused, and patted the little heir's curly head.

"You ride a horse every day, don't you, Mr. Withers?"

"Yes."

"Its nice, isn't it? Why don't you speak," pursued the child. "You look as if you were going to cry. Margaret cries often."

Paul's heart leaped. "Does she? Why?"

"Something about, I don't know," said Cecil, with a puzzled look. "I think its about Scotland."

Paul's jealous heart suggested a Scotch lover immediately. "Well, good bye," said he, striving to speak gaily.

"Good bye," said the boy, looking wistfully after him.

Paul rode off hastily, his heart more in a flame, his brain more in a whirl than ever. His passion was a mystery to himself. Literally, he knew nothing of Margaret Percy. He had never heard her speak, save commonplace words. He was ignorant of her inward self, of her soul, of her quality of mind even. He was in love with a faultless form, and a white chiselled face, and two blue eyes, and a voice of marvellous sweetness. The words this voice uttered were nothing in themselves. He had never heard this girl express a sentiment or a feeling. He had only heard her calm allusions to the weather, or her state of health. Even in that terrible moment when the waves were gathering round her, the only passion she had seemed capable of was scorn, or dread that he had come to share the death she was so calmly waiting for. Afterwards, when he had saved her, she had coolly referred him for thanks to her father. And he was mad enough to love this bloodless, soulless being; to invest her with attributes that perhaps did not of right belong to her. Why did he love her?

He walked his horse slowly down the avenue, his eyes lowered, his face pale. Presently he found himself stopped by a little gate which crossed the path, and on the other side of this gate was a young girl, mounted on a fine horse. In her black hat, falling feather, and long, sweeping riding dress, this girl looked like the sweet vignette of some painter's fancy.

Shaded by the drooping branches of the beech trees, tinted with the first gold of the autumn, with her horse drawn up on the deep green aftermath of the park, she waited while Paul descended from his horse and unfastened the gate. It had stuck, or the iron was rusty. Anyhow, it took him some time; and meanwhile he gazed his fill upon the young face before him. I think that it is not true that when one is in love it renders one indifferent to all the faces that one meets; because, if the soul is engrossed with one image, if one name is ever trembling on the lips, if the fond, yearning heart is for ever repeating the last treasured looks and words of the loved one, and the whole inward being is given up passionately to the contemplation of one existence, that is only one reason why we should feel anxious to consult every circumstance, person, or thing, which may bear remotely on the subject of our thoughts.

Paul Withers, a man of the people, loved Margaret Percy, a young and lovely woman of the aristocracy; and now chance had thrown in his way a being of the same order to which Margaret belonged—young, lovely, and highly born. Paul looked at her curiously. Abundance of fair hair fell profusely round the face, and it was a face like unto an angel's. Perhaps, if the features had been compared with those of Miss Percy, the palm for mere regularity of outline might have been awarded to her; but here, if it existed at all, the superiority ceased. The hazel eyes were joyous and brilliant, soft and beautiful, the complexion delicate as a rose leaf, a rich bloom on the cheeks; but about the mouth it was that the peculiar charm rested. I cannot explain it. It was indefinable; but it was spiritual. Words of eloquence flowed easily from those lips; but of that Paul knew nothing. He only saw the blooming face, the falling brown hair, the divine expression, and then he began to wonder where he had seen a like face before. It was as though one of the angels from the paintings

of the old masters had come down to this
nineteenth century life of ours. Yes, he
had somewhere seen such a face. Amid
the clouds of fire and purple above where
the pale form was stretched on the cross?
and the drooped figures of the women were
bending towards the earth? Or was it in the
grey dawning of the day, when the anxious
watchers questioned eagerly, with the back
ground of morning mist, and the roofs of
the yet sleeping city dimly visible, had he
seen one clothed in white, sitting on a
sepulchre; and was this the face of the
angel? One thing was certain. Centuries
ago some inspired painter had pictured the
very face which now beamed on Paul. He
could not remember where or when he
had seen it; but when the girl courte-
ously thanked him, turned her horse's
head and rode off, Paul felt refreshed, as
though a voice had cheered him and whispered hope to him. He was at that time a
dreaming creature, and he never thought of
inquiring the name of this vision of beauty.

It satisfied him to think that he had gazed on her; and he rode on with the tumult in his soul quelled, and a feeling of strange peace at his heart. He almost believed that he had really gazed on the face of an angel.

CHAPTER II.

EMMA.

THE sun was sinking towards the west
when Paul came in sight of Roggmoore
Lodge. He drew up his horse, and looked
at it. The lawn was level, and of a
vivid green. The autumn flowers bloomed
brightly. Against the house the monthly
roses trailed. Many of their leaves lay
scattered on the path. The large trees
rustled, and whispered mysteriously, and
the little pleasant white house seemed to
nestle securely amongst them. Albert came
out in front when he saw Paul. He went
to him.

"What are you looking at, Paul?"

"At your house."

"Pretty, unpretending little place. Is it not?" said Albert. "I could be very happy there for one, with a wife that I loved."

"You with a wife?" said Paul, with a glance at the slight boyish form.

"Why not?"

"Too young to know anything about love," said Paul, decidedly.

Albert blushed. "Great geniuses," said he, diffidently, "experience love at an early age. Byron, you know, was in love at eight years old, and Danté—or was it Tasso?"

"I don't remember," said Paul, slashing at the branches of the trees, "and," he added roughly, "I don't care."

"Paul, you are vexed at something. You are cross."

"Am I?"

"Yes. You look tired, and you answer snappishly."

"I am very sorry. Good evening. I must go now," and he began to draw up the reins of his horse.

"You're not going without seeing your mother and sister. We were just going to tea. Emma and I have been gathering plums all the afternoon, for your mother to make preserves with to-morrow. Come in. It's the last opportunity you will have, for some time to come, of witnessing and enjoying our simple country life here, for to-night my grand brother Charles is coming down, and he'll be here some weeks."

"To-night?"

"Yes."

Paul got off his horse, and began to lead him towards the stable. "Charles is 'un homme comme il faut.' He rises at nine, breakfasts at ten. His valet dresses him, his groom rides behind him. He dines at eight. He reads German, and smokes recherché cheroots afterwards, unless some of the county gentlemen dine with him. Charles would be shocked at my picking fruit, and

dining at one. He thinks me a little un-
taught brute."

"He is, then, very aristocratic in his
notions?"

"Immensely so."

"Well, he has rank, and he has wealth.
He has a right to be as haughty as he
pleases."

"I can't see that. Look at Margaret
Percy, for instance."

Paul's cheek burned consciously, but
young Roggmoore did not notice it, and
continued—

"There's Margaret Percy—pretty enough
and amiable enough, and a good girl after
all, but I think I should like to address her
in the words of Madame de Maintenon,—
'Je ne suis pas prévenus contre vous mais
je vois dans vous un orgueil effroyable.'
Margaret thinks that all in the middle
ranks are made of something different to
herself."

"As you belong to the same set as Miss
Percy," said Paul, "I suppose you mean *me*

to understand that I ought to be penetrated with gratitude at *your* wonderful condescension."

" Paul, you are certainly out of humour, and you are unjust. What am I ? The youngest of three sons. Nothing in the great world, I assure you. Don't talk nonsense."

So Paul was silent; and when he had seen to the wants of his horse, he went into the garden to look for Emma. He found her buried among the plum trees; two large baskets filled with purple fruit stood near her on the grass. She wore a straw hat and a print dress, and a pair of garden gloves lay near her. She raised her head when she heard his step, and gave a quick glance from her dark bright eyes; her cheek was hot and flushed.

" Paul !"

" Emma !"

He threw himself on the grass at her feet and turned his face away.

" Emma ?"

" Yes, Paul."

"Mr. Roggmoore is coming to-night."

"I know."

"I hope he will tell you how long your suspense is to last."

"Why?" she spoke pettishly.

"He has no right to keep you any longer in this uncertain state. I believe he means you wrong; I do, on my soul."

"And you have never seen him," scornfully.

"No, but his brother tells me that he is a most haughty being. Is it likely that he means to marry his housekeeper's daughter?"

"Paul, I thought you and I had settled that question long ago."

"No, you used some high flown words, Emma, and talked me down, and tried to make me ashamed of myself. You shall not do so again. Since then, I have seen something more of these great people, to whose set your lover belongs, and I can pretty well judge in what light Charles Bingham Roggmoore, Esq., regards you."

She drew on her gloves.

"Will you help me to carry these fruit baskets into the house?" said she, coldly.

"No, I won't. I mean you to talk to me again about this man, and to explain everything. If you don't, I'll remain here until he comes to-night, and then I'll ask him his intentions."

She grew a little pale. "Do so by all means, and get horsewhipped for your insolence."

Paul laughed bitterly, but he did not speak. Emma took up one basket of fruit. It was heavy. It slipped, and half its contents were spilt. Paul, who had not stirred from his place on the ground, began to pick up the plums, and replace them in the basket.

"I suppose you have made no confidant of Albert Roggmoore?"

"I have had too severe a lesson on the making of confidants, Paul Withers."

"You mean that my interference is so disagreeable to you?"

"Yes, I do. You express my meaning perfectly."

"Emma, do you love this man wholly and solely for himself alone, or because he is Charles Bingham Roggmoore, Esq. Does no ambition mingle with your love?"

"I cannot see what right you have to question me."

"Emma," said Paul, tenderly, "you are my sister, and I love you. Your honour is very dear to me."

"Be completely at your ease. I am the fittest guardian of my own honour."

"I know you think so; but may not love blind you? If ambition sways you, then I may leave you to guard your own honour; but if you love, really love, it is a different thing. Love is a sweet poison, Emma."

"Be it so. I would rather die a sweet death, by so sweet a poison, than linger out a long barren life of loneliness."

"What do you mean?" and Paul started, and turned deadly white.

"Do be at your ease," said Emma, scornfully. "I have not forfeited my claims to this base world's respect. Je suis sans tache et sans reproche, Paul."

"Thank God for that. But Emma, why will you quarrel with me? Why this bitterness, this scorn?"

"You can never comprehend my feelings.

"It is not given to a nature like yours to fathom the depths of a nature like mine."

"Not given."

"No. You are cool, calm, prudent, industrious, business like. I am 'a child of the sun.' When I read the lines of the bride of Abydos, I think I must belong to those southern climes. My nature is a fire, my heart is a flame. Don't laugh," and she turned the full gaze of her dark eyes on Paul.

"I am not inclined to laugh, Emma; you speak earnestly; you are not acting. Then you really love this Roggmoore?"

"More than my life, more than my hopes of salvation. I love him to the exclusion of every other feeling. I could slay the woman on whom he should cast his eye: I could slay myself if I found him false or faithless. Oh, Paul, I do not know what fate means, by giving me only you, with your stern, calm face and well-regulated feelings for a listener. A sympathizer you can never be."

"Emma, there is unrest in your eye; you begin to doubt this high born lover."

"I—Yes." She was pale; she took off her hat and sunk on the ground. "Do I show uneasiness, anxiety, dread in my face?"

"Yes, Emma."

"Oh, Paul! if you could sympathise—if you could feel as I feel, it would so comfort me to tell you; but you have no pity, none."

"Emma, will it comfort you to learn that I too love deeply, passionately."

"You, Paul?"

"Yes; and I have no hope in my love; the object of it is too far above me for me even to breathe her name."

"Like the lover in the German song,"

said Emma, smiling a little. "Oh, Paul, if you have never *possessed* there is nothing to lose. I have enjoyed the happiness of loving and being loved; now, as Schiller says, perhaps it is time for me to die; I have lived long enough."

"You harass me terribly, Emma. You speak as though you were lost."

"I am not; my honour is untouched, but my love is terrible, my jealousy wakeful. Paul, if you could know all you would see that I suffer."

"Tell all then, Emma, I entreat, I implore you."

"Where's Paul," said the voice of Mrs. Withers.

"Emma, have you gathered the plums?"

Emma did not answer.

Mrs. Withers came upon them.

Paul rose and embraced his mother.

"My boy, I couldn't think where you were gone. Tea is ready. Come, my dear," to Emma.

Emma rose smilingly. "We can send

the servants for the fruit, I suppose," she said; but Paul and his mother carried the baskets of fruit between them.

"All tea time poor Mrs. Withers was busied in descanting on the idleness and sudden love of finery in Jane, the housemaid. She knew not what storms were brewing in the breasts of her son and daughter. Emma sat with changing cheek, and anxious starting at every sound. Paul was moody and watchful, and a slow resentful fire burnt in his eye. Albert talked and laughed incessantly. After tea, Paul embraced his mother and sister, and then he went for his horse. The sun had gone down, and it was in the autumn twilight that he left the white house, amidst the whispering trees, and turned his horse's head towards Aberglace.

CHAPTER III.

CHARLES BINGHAM ROGGMOORE.

AND the twilight deepened, and the night
wind arose, and went sighing through the
branches, and wailing at the casements
mournfully. The seared leaves fell on the
grass paths. The roses swayed their gentle
heads to and fro, and their soft leaves
showered thickly down; and still the tall
trees whispered and rustled, and then a
light shone brightly in the window of the
white house. They were preparing for the
coming of the master. A supper was laid
out for him. Spotless linen was spread on

the table. Silver and crystal gleamed brightly. A fire was kindled. The couch was drawn up to it.

Mrs. Withers and Jane were busy below. Albert was lolling by the fire mending his fishing lines, and greatly in Mrs. Withers's way. And Emma, she had changed her dress for one of dark silk. Her hair was wound gracefully about her head, a falling collar of white lace was round her throat. Emma, the untidy of Portarlington Place, was no more. She had merged into Emma the coquette. She had twisted one rich, red rose amid her bright tresses. And the housekeeper's daughter lounged on a couch by the fire in the dining-room, with a book of poems in her hand; but she did not read. She watched, and waited patiently. She rose and walked to the window. The harvest moon had risen, and her soft, rich light illumined the autumn garden, and glanced on the swaying boughs of the trees; and Emma stole out into the night, and went down the gravel path, and to-

c 2

wards the gate, and there she watched and waited. resently she Pheard the hoofs of a horse battering against the mountain road-way, and now the horseman came in sight. He was climbing slowly the ascent of the path, and Emma ran on to meet him. She spoke thickly, breathlessly, "Charles."

He stopped his horse. "Who is this? Emma? Mon Dieu!"

"Oh, Charles! six weeks and you have not written."

He took her hand, stooped down, and kissed her cheek. "My time has been so taken up."

"Taken up. Oh, Charles! and have you no pity for me, waiting always for a letter that never came? It was cruel, cruel."

"Dieu merci! this is pleasant. When I come here to get rest and quiet, to be greeted by reproaches and whines. Let me alone for to-night. I am tired. To-morrow you shall complain to your heart's content."

She walked quietly by the side of his

horse up the steep ascent of the path, and spoke not a word. Neither did Mr. Roggmoore

In silence they entered the grounds. Then Emma ran on first and seated herself again in the dining-room, and Mr. Roggmoore came round to the stable and shouted to the groom. He had left his own groom and valet at Aberglace that night. They would come in the morning. Then there was a hurry, and a bustle, and a supper, of which he partook alone.

Afterwards Emma, who had gone to her own room, went unbidden into the parlour. Charles Bingham Roggmoore and Albert were chatting and smoking together.

"Come in, Miss Withers," said Albert, gaily.

And Miss Withers went in. The lamp light fell upon a fair, flushed face, a dark, restless eye, on a young and handsome woman. With it all, and though she had come into the presence of the young men, there was nothing that could be termed bold about Emma. Haughty, fierce, passionate; but still feminine. An impetuous, fiery woman; but a woman still. She entered the dining parlour. "I've come to say good night, gentlemen."

"If our smoking does not inconvenience you, remain a few moments, Miss Withers," said the elder Roggmoore.

And Emma remained.

Then he talked about horseflesh, and sporting, and fishing, rents, drains, and mortgages to his brother.

Emma did not take the hint. She sat still and waited. Ten o'clock struck. Then she rose and wished the brothers good night, and climbed to her own chamber. She locked the door, flung herself on the bed, and moaned piteously. Then she rose and paced her room. He is tired of me. He would be rid of me. There is some other face which he pursues. Charles Roggmoore, I will find out this new toy. I will whisper in her ear, and be revenged. This spring, only this last spring, I would have staked my soul on his faith; but six weeks' silence; and to-night he is cold, changed, brutal. She sat down moodily.

Just then there came a ráp at the door. "Emma, my dear, let me in. You're not in bed."

"I can't, mamma."

"Yes, yes. I want to speak to you particularly."

So Emma let her in.

The mother stood aghast at her daughter's white, agonised face. "What is the matter?"

"Nothing."

"You look dreadfully."

"Oh, I have a headache."

"Tell your mother what grieves you. Mr. Roggmoore is unkind, I suppose."

"What is Mr. Roggmoore to me?"

"I'm not a fool," said Mrs. Withers, angrily. "Can't I see that you are in love with each other."

"You see what no one else sees. You see what you wish to see. I'm only the daughter of Mr. Roggmoore's house-keeper."

"No matter. You are the most beauti-ful girl in the county, and your mind is well cultivated. You are quite his equal."

"Don't talk nonsense, mother."

"Yes, all I say is nonsense; and there you go on hiding things from me, instead of confiding in your mother. How can I act when I know nothing?"

"Heaven knows, I don't want you to act."

"Then why do you go on fretting, and looking ill? And why have you lost your appetite? Why are you always out of temper? If nothing is the matter, why can't you laugh and be cheerful like other girls?"

"I wish you would let me go to sleep, mother. My head is bad."

"Is it? Well, let me see you in bed first."

Emma grumbled, but submitted.

Mrs. Withers was a tender mother. She

smoothed the pillows, kissed the hot fore-head of her daughter, and left her; but Emma did not sleep all the night. She talked to herself, and moaned with the pain of her wounded, despairing love. She did not weep. Tears refused to come to her hot, dry eyes. Towards morning she slept in spite of herself.

Her mother awakened her. She set the breakfast tray on the bed. " Emma, get up and take a cup of tea."

Emma raised her head, which now really ached sadly. "Thank you, mother."

" You have slept late. It is ten o'clock, and both the gentlemen are gone to pay an early visit, and, I think, to spend the day out."

" Where ?"

" At Percy Priory."

" Oh, with those hateful, proud Percies. She sat up and ate a bit of toast, and sipped her tea.

Mrs. Withers sat by her side.

" I can't bear that Miss Percy, with he·

white, cold face. I remember speaking to
her once on the beach at Aberglace, when
we first came down here. I was a little
idiot then, and I had heard so much of
these great Percies ; and one of the Perfectways pointed her out to me, sitting near the
sea with her maid, and I went up and
said, 'What a pretty place this is,' and she
looked at her maid as though she was
astonished at *my* daring to speak to her.
She was only about fourteen then ; but the
maid answered for her. 'Yes, its a fine
place,' she said, and then she and Miss
Percy got up and moved away. I have
always hated that girl since."

"I'll get you another cup of tea," said
Mrs. Withers. When she returned with
the tea Mrs. Withers looked flushed.
" Paul been again."

" Paul !"

" Yes. He's going on again to Percy
Priory. Miss Percy is in delicate health."

" Bother Miss Percy."

" Paul will call here again to see you

when he returns, if your head isn't better."

"Very well." Emma laid down again, and closed her eyes. "I shall try and sleep," she said, glad of a chance of being alone; and she lay all the day with closed eyes in a half dreamy state, glad of the bodily pain which diverted her thoughts from the sharper pain within.

Paul rode on through the autumn day. In some places the corn yet stood uncut, for the harvest was late in those mountains; in others it was bound into yellow sheaves. The September sunlight streamed over mountain side and woodland. The air was soft, balmy, delicious. The sweet influence of the day was about Paul's soul. He did not feel swayed by such a tempest of passion as he had done the day before.

At the place where the mountain path sloped down towards the grim dwelling of Madame Williams he paused, and walked his horse slowly. The trouble the old lady hinted at is come upon me, thought

Paul.   Suppose I were to go down and tell
her how much I love Miss Percy. He
smiled a little at the absurd thought, and
then urged his horse on more swiftly.

Once more the Percy woods, once more
the pretty lodge gates, once more the lordly
park for a long mile, and then the great
house, and the servant who held his horse ;
and Paul crosses the marble hall, and is
shewn this time into the gorgeous dining-
room, as he was on the first occasion of his
visit to Percy Priory. It was empty ; but
there lay the book with the name written
in it. He did not dare to touch it. Presently there entered a lady whom Paul had
never seen before, a middle-aged person,
of good family and small means, who acted
as *chaperone* to Miss Percy.

Mrs. Avenel introduced herself, and
asked Paul to be seated. "Miss Percy is
much better. She is in the garden." And
presently Miss Percy came in, lovelier, so
Paul thought, than any poet's dream.

Margaret Percy could   not but have

noticed that the young surgeon's cheek changed whenever she appeared. She could not but have noticed it; because she always condescended to fix her deep blue eyes upon him when first he entered her presence. Now his face was in a flame. It grew pale when he felt her pulse, and his voice trembled. She saw it, and knew it all.

"Did you take the draught, Miss Percy?"

"Yes, and I feel much better. Much better."

"You need not renew it then."

"Very well, Mr. Withers."

Still commonplace, every day words, quiet replies—mere nothings she had uttered, and still Paul loved her.

"Here comes Charles," said Mrs. Avenel, and Charles came in. Paul looked up at him.

Charles Bingham Roggmoore was a young man of six and twenty. The stamp of high birth and refinement was impressed upon him. He stood six feet. His complexion was fair, his features regular, his hair light. He wore no whiskers, only a small silky moustache. His favourite haunt was Paris. His manners, his ideas, his tone altogether had taken a foreign tinge. Ancient as was his name, enormous as were his possessions, Charles Bingham Roggmoore had slight affection for his country. His mother had been educated in France, and from her her eldest son had imbibed his foreign tastes. She was still alive, residing at Versailles. Charles Bingham was the owner of three large estates. He was heir to an earldom, between which and himself there was only the life of a feeble old uncle.

He was a polished patrician, placid in his manners, and to him Emma Withers had declared herself affianced. It was impossible, Paul felt; and while he looked at the pink and white complexion, and noted the delicate hand, which would have delighted Byron, he muttered, " This is a

being to win a lady's heart; this is the
soft, perfumed homme comme il fault, with
faultless kid gloves and perfect boots," and
Paul recognised him.

The last time he had looked upon the
fair face of this gentleman was in Burdett
Court, in the New Cut, when poor, shivering, miserable Grace had cowered at his
feet in that den of infamy and poverty.
Poor Grace, who now slept in her pauper's
grave, unwept, unknown, unpitied; and
this man, who had embittered her existence, and destroyed her purity, stood
serenely smiling in the splendid salon of
the Percys, with his gaze fixed on Margaret, that peerless lady who was his
equal, and whom he had a right to gaze
upon. He did not recognise Paul. He
had scarcely noticed the dark-haired young
surgeon. He never thought of him from
the time when he had left him in that
wretched room until now. But Paul knew
him for a libertine, a smooth, suave, smiling libertine, whose passions did not burn

less fiercely for being veiled beneath a polished surface. He thought of Emma, and the lurid fire in his eyes burnt fiercely. Was he leading her politely also towards a death of shame, and a pauper's burial?

"Honest, though poor," muttered Paul, as he mounted his horse. "She was honest, God help her, before she came into this cursed country. But if he has wronged her, he shall answer for it to me out here in the mountain path, hand to hand, and man to man," and Paul smiled grimly. He rode those sixteen miles, which took him to Roggmoore Lodge, he knew not how. He took his horse round to the stable, and then sought his mother. He found her up to the elbows in preserves and plums.

"Mother, I want to see Emma."

"She's asleep now."

"Never mind, she must awaken."

"What's the matter?"

"Nothing. At least, it is a message I

must give her alone. I must, indeed, mother. Let me see her."

" Whatever is it ?"

" Mother, it is a secret. I must not tell it to any one but Emma."

So Mrs. Withers took Paul to Emma's bed side, and aroused her, and then stood by to hear the secret.

" Go away, mother," said Paul. " Upon my honour, I dare not say what I have to say to any one but Emma."

Paul was dreadfully excited, and he blundered, as excited people do. Emma, with more ready tact, came to his aid.

" I know what it is," she said. " It's that message from ——. Indeed, mother, you must not hear. It's a little secret of our own."

So they got rid of their mother, and then Paul bent down and whispered his secret into Emma's ear. To his surprise, she manifested no concern.

" Well, Paul, is that all ?"

" All, Emma. Does it not terrify

you to find in whose hands your fate lies ?"

" No. Your tale is nothing. All men do these things, if silly peasant girls will listen to them."

" All men ?   Do I ?"

" You. Oh, you are poor. You have your character to keep up."

"Emma, I fear you are corrupt at heart."

At those words, Emma flushed hotly.

" Don't say such things, Paul. But I have read books, and have talked to Charles—Mr. Roggmoore, I mean—and I believe men of the aristocracy are very dissipated."

" Will you tell me how you stand with this man ? I *will* learn. I intend to meet him on his return home, and to charge him with his perfidy."

Emma rose in the bed, and laid her hand on Paul's arm. " Don't, Paul, don't. I swear to you solemnly that he has done me no wrong. I love him perhaps too much, but he has never wronged me."

"He wishes to, then?"

"No. He would not oppose my leaving him to-morrow."

"Emma, there is mystery here. Why will you not tell me all?"

"Give me a month?"

"No. In a month your ruin may be sealed."

"A week then?"

"Well, I will give you a week. But remember, if by that time my doubts are not cleared up, I shall have a fierce account to settle with Charles Bingham Rogg-moore."

CHAPTER IV.

THE WEEK.

MARGARET Percy and Charles Bingham
Roggmoore remained standing in the window which looked out upon the flower
garden. That wide green garden, with its
wealth of autumn blossoms, was a fair sight
on a bright morning, but the young man
looked earnestly into the girl's beautiful
face, and she lowered her eyes, and seemed
half conscious of the purpose of his unspoken thoughts. No word passed between
them, until at last Charles Roggmoore said,
in his soft musical voice, " Margaret."

" Yes."

" No need for me to plead my cause in mere words. You know that you hold my life in the hollow of your hand."

" Your life ?"

" All that makes life worth anything."

A slight curve of the lip was unnoticed by Mr. Roggmoore, but she did not speak then. He went on again.

" I am no eloquent pleader, Margaret. No poet, to amuse you with sweet similitudes, or fiery flights of passion and pathos. I am a man, with a man's heart. I have only some short simple words at my command. I love you, but I cannot tell you so in poetical strain."

Had he reckoned on her light mockery of his wooing, and did he wisely try to put it out of her power to despise a love so earnestly and simply urged ? Still Margaret remained silent.

" Margaret, you will not speak ? What am I to infer ? Is all hope over for me ?"

Then the self-same blush which had

warmed her cheek at Paul's question mounted to it again, but her blue eyes shot out an angry glance, and she said—

"Mr. Roggmoore, this is all acting. I don't approve of acting. My father told me only last night of your intended visit, and also that he had apprised you of my complete submission to his wishes. Eloquent pleading would indeed be thrown away on one who is already signed, sealed, and delivered to you. I want no poetry, no pathos. I am to be your wife, and have agreed to submit."

He bit his lip, and a slight expletive escaped him.

"Diable, mademoiselle, you do not flatter."

"Neither do I wish that *you* should, Mr. Roggmoore."

"Oh, then our courtship is to be bereft of even the semblance of love, Margaret. I am not to address you in a fond tone. I am only to talk of the weather, the last opera, or the county gossip. I am never to presume on my sweet privilege, and to treat you as my affianced bride."

"Situated as we are, perfectly comprehending, both of us, that this is a mariage de convenance, why need we lend ourselves to a hollow mockery? You obtain my large Scotch estates, and you know well that your escutcheon will not be stained by an alliance with Cecil Percy's only daughter. I take my stand as Mrs. Charles Bingham Roggmoore. Our united wealth will prove a colossal fortune. You have blue blood also. One day you will be Earl Danvers. I could not please my dear father better than by accepting you. I have accepted you."

"Thank you, sweet Margaret. So rich and rare a gift must make me grateful; but there is poison in my cup of happiness. You detest me, Margaret."

"A strong word, Mr. Roggmoore."

"Not stronger than my feelings on the subject. You talk of your Scotch estates, and your good birth. Do you think I value you only for these ?"

" No. I am reckoned beautiful; and you think I should grace your drawing-rooms in St. James's Square."

" Vraiment, Margaret! you are original."

" Because I say I am reckoned beautiful ? I have been told so every day ever since I can remember."

" Sans doûte; and now listen to me, Marguerite des Marguerites. I love you intensely. I worship you. If you could be divested of your wealth, your name, still I would offer you my hand and my heart. Do you believe this ?"

" No."

" Obdurate marble, cruel," said Charles, passionately, and the blood mounted into his fair face. " When you are my wife—"

" Until then reserve your rhapsodies," interrupted Margaret, placidly. " I am going now to prepare for a ride," and she went immediately from the room.

" Petite diâble!" exclaimed Charles, when

left alone. " I wish I did only care for her social advantages ; but with all her durête, her coldness, I almost worship her. Will it last, I wonder ? I hope so. After marriage the little wild cat will be tamed ; and I need never be jealous, for her inordinate pride will be her complete safeguard, and she has never passed one season in London. She loves no one else. Yes, I will teach her to love me before I have done with her. What a perfect face it is ; and what repose of manner, even when most roused. What a difference to those great, dark eyes, and hot, flushed cheeks, and tearing passions of— Pah ! I hate her name. After all there *is* no true sympathy between patrician and plebeian. I have been a consummate ass." And then Charles Roggmoore opened the French window, and walked out into the mellow, September sunshine ; and the cool breeze fanned his brow, and he grew calmer.

In the solitude of her luxurious chamber sat Margaret Percy, plunged amid the soft cushions of an ottoman, her head buried in her hands.

"Presently there came a knock at the door. "It is I, Margaret," said a sweet voice. "May I come in?"

"Oh yes, Flora. Come in," and Flora came in.

The reader would recognise her at once. It was the same blooming face which had rivetted Paul Withers's gaze in the park the day before; the same golden, brown hair; even the same dark hat, and drooping feather. She was a creature full of grace, was Flora Heartley. Every action was airy, unstudied, flexile. Eighteen summers had shed their suns on her bright, young head. Eighteen summers had she rejoiced the hearts of her parents, of all who came within her benign influence. She came up to Margaret Percy, stooped, and touched the white, smooth brow with her rosy lips, then sunk down by her side.

"Sad, Margaret?"

"Yes."

"Why?"

"Need you ask?"

"Well, I suppose I can guess;" and she wound her arm fondly round Miss Percy's waist. The latter suffered her caresses, but did not respond to them in any way.

At last she said, suddenly, and averting her face, "Flora, I feel very wretched."

"I wish I could comfort you."

"So you do in a manner. I like to feel your fresh pink soft palm pressed to my hot forehead. I like to hear your voice, it calms me like solemn music."

"How complimentary!"

"No; you know I never flatter."

"I am glad if my hands and my voice can work such miracles."

They sat still a few moments. At last Margaret got up and paced the room huriedly. "Flora, I must act before the world, I will not before you. I am to marry Charles Bingham Roggmoore, and I detest him."

"Then why marry him?"

"How easy to ask, how difficult to make you understand my answer. You can never comprehend my motives, Flora."

"No?"

"No. You see," she went on hurriedly, "the elements of which our natures are composed are diametrically opposite. You live for the next world, I live for this."

"Admitting that, I cannot see how you can further your interests in this world by joining yourself to a person you abhor."

"There it is," said Margaret, pressing her hands tightly together, and coming to a stand in her hurried walk. "There it is. You cannot understand, sweet, rosy, innocent child; pure, transparent soul; lofty, high-toned mind. You are as much above me in your grand simplicity, in your unswerving perception of right and wrong. Your unselfish nature is as much superior to mine in magnitude, as the great ocean is superior to the little stream that runs there at the foot of those pollard willows," pointing towards the window.

"You are too hard on yourself, flatterer," said Flora, playfully. "A good motive lies at the roots of your actions—obedience to your father."

"Well, yes, that is true ; but still I am bound to say that I love rank, power, place. I shall glory in being the wife of the richest earl in England. You cannot understand that, Flora ?"

"No. I can understand wishing to be the wife of the greatest statesman, the greatest author, the greatest poet. Still better can I understand wishing to be the wife of the person I love."

"Don't talk nonsense and soft sentiment, Flora. It is unworthy of your intellect and mind."

"Is love all nonsense in your opinion, Miss Percy ?"

"Yes, Miss Heartley," said Margaret, laughing a little, then seating herself. "Why do you turn your great solemn eyes on me, little one, as though I had said there was no heaven ?"

"Love is heaven, and heaven is love, Margaret."

"So some foolish rhymster has said, child; but I choose to doubt his pretty assertion. At least here, in this nether world, the less such silly sentimentality is preached the better. So, please, don't choose that for your text if you mean to give me a sermon."

"What for my text?"

"Love."

"Its all nonsense, then?"

"All," said Miss Percy, emphatically. Every bit, Flora."

"Very well," said Flora, smiling. "Then give me your reasons for believing, or rather for disbelieving."

"Willingly. Listen. I see two people who are said to be in love. They go on in the orthodox style. Mind, I take a perfectly unexceptionable pair. The lover sighs, and looks, and loves, and pours forth rhapsodies; and the lady will not unsought be won, &c., and she manages 'de cacher

son amour' for a time, though she tells her
confidential friend how useless life would
be without the beloved one—I think that
is the proper phrase. At last she consents,
and they are wed, and the bells ring, and
the mother weeps; and the lovely bride-
maids, and their white silks, and blush
roses, have honourable mention in the newspapers; and there are loads of carriages,
and coronets, if you like, and limitless
bridecake, and 'unvalued jewels,' as poor
Clarence says; and then the pair whirl off,
and they fly on the wings of love to the
continent. There, no doubt, they find it
delightful; especially if they have no accident with the luggage, and if the cook-
ing is always good. Well, they come
back, and settle down to their round
of visiting, and riding, and opera going.
The husband goes into parliament, and
in the recess he attends to his estates. Two years after marriage, what
do you suppose those people care for each
other?"

"A great deal, I hope."

"Do you? Well, four years after, what do they care?"

"Still a great deal."

"Ten years, gentle Flora, what then?"

"Still much. Much, I should hope, Margaret. Passion will have spread his wings and flown; but love, steadfast, will remain, holy and lovely, as the light of a pure summer moon which succeeds to the hot glare of the day-god."

"A cool simile, Flora. A wonderful cooling down, even you admit, when you choose moonlight after sunlight. Does not some poet say, 'All thy passions matched with mine, are as moonlight unto sunlight, as water unto wine?'"

"Yes. Tennyson, in 'Locksley Hall.' But I did not think of that."

"No. But why not go on, and say that the married love of ten years is like a stream of cold clear water, whereas the un-married love of three months is like the sparkling, rosy, exhilarating fruit of the vine, eh ?"

"You mock, Margaret."

"Yes, I can't help it. All this stuff about love annoys me. It never lasts, Flora—it never lasts."

"If you are really to marry Mr. Rogg-moore, Margaret, perhaps it is as well that you should continue in your disbelief?"

"What do you mean ?" asked Miss Percy, almost sharply.

"I only mean, dear girl, that it would be a sad thing if, when irrevocably pledged to him, some magician should arise, who would have power to stir your nature to its utmost depths."

"Poor child. I have no depths in my nature. I am altogether cold, perfectly heartless, terribly unromantic, Flora."

"If so, why do you dislike the idea of marrying this gentleman ? You disbelieve in love; you believe in worldly greatness as a means of contentment. This worldly greatness is within your reach. Accept

what fate offers you of good at (least in
your eyes), and don't be so cast down."

"Flora, you probe me terribly. If I
have, or had, a weak place in my nature,
you would find it out. But, thank Heaven,
I have not."

"Very well, Margaret. Then there is an
end to the matter."

"With all my heart. Let us talk of
something else. Will you come for a ride
with me, Flora?"

Flora agreed, and a few minutes later
found the ladies mounted on their prancing
horses, and escorted by Charles Bingham
Roggmoore, setting out from the house for
a ride. Charles Bingham looked perfect,
mounted on a "gallant grey," booted, spur-
red, gloved, to most excellent advantage.
His light hair and silky moustache curled
to admiration, his "tout ensemble" faultless,
his smile charming, his voice like music,
and he bowed, and flattered, and behaved
himself "comme ordinaire," as a man of
fashion and of the world.

The ride lasted long, and it was not till twilight that the trio returned to Percy Priory. Flora was to remain to dinner and to sleep. A servant was despatched to the rectory, where dwelt her father, to bring her a suitable dress, and the two girls entered the dining room at seven, the dinner hour, each dressed in a characteristic style, each one ravishingly lovely. Margaret wore a dress of ruby-coloured velvet, which contrasted well with her snowy neck and arms, and amid her rich brown tresses were twined some choice hothouse flowers, of mingled white and crimson. Her face was not quite so pale as ordinary. A faint rose tinged her cheek, and an unwonted fire gleamed in her blue eyes. She sat and smiled, and talked brilliantly.

Flora, with her brown hair, glowing cheeks, and style of loveliness, at once Hebe-like and angelic, was of a brighter beauty than the statue-like Margaret. She wore a dress of white lace, with no ornament of any kind. Cecil Percy sat stately, at the head of his table, and behaved with perfect politeness to everybody. But it was not a gay party. Afterwards, the ladies escaped to the drawing room, and the gentlemen were left alone. Then Cecil Percy unbent a little.

" Well, Charles, is it concluded ?"

" Yes, Mr. Percy. Margaret promised me this morning to be my wife, but she grudges me the splendid gift."

" Hah," said Mr. Percy, dividing a fine bunch of grapes with his white refined fingers. " Grudges, did you say ?"

" Heartily, Mr. Percy."

" Stuff," said Mr. Percy, pulling the grapes from the stalk. " Stuff, my dear friend. This is an alliance on which I have set my heart. It is perfectly unexceptionable in every way. All sides are delighted. And not only that, but in tastes, in feelings, you are well suited. Each knows the value of the other. Each must be inwardly convinced that he or she could not possibly do better. There is, therefore, nothing more to be said. And now shake hands with me, Charles, as my future son-in-law."

They clasped hands.

"And have you fixed any time, Charles?"

"No. I should wish it settled as soon as possible, but I fear much Margaret will hold me off for a long time."

"You must use all your arts of persuasion."

"I?"

"Yes."

"I have not an iota of influence with Miss Percy," said Charles, a little bitterly.

Mr. Percy scarcely noticed the annoyance of his guest. In the code of principles which guided his actions, passion, I had almost said feeling, had no place. He could not comprehend how Charles could feel annoyed at Margaret's coldness. Margaret, who had promised to be his wife.

"Shall we adjourn," said Mr. Percy, and they adjourned.

The next day, early, Flora Heartley stole down stairs long before any of the pampered servants were afoot, and pushed open the door of the library. She walked up to the book shelves, and began to look through some of the volumes, when the door opened softly. She turned, and found herself face to face with Charles Bingham Roggmoore. He was serene and smiling, but there was a most unpleasant light in his eye.

"Good morning, sweet Queen of Flowers," said he, gaily.

Flora took his pleasantry with perfect good temper and good faith. She hoped he had slept well.

"No. I have not closed an eye all night."

Flora said she was sorry.

"How very kind of you, Miss Heartley."

There was a slight tone of mockery in the words. Flora glanced up brightly at him with an inquiring eye and a heightened colour.

"How good of Miss Heartley to express regret at anything that Charles Bingham Roggmoore suffers."

"What does Mr. Roggmoore wish me to understand," asked Flora, firmly.

"The person whom you honour by addressing, Miss Heartley, has but one meaning, and he wishes to convey it to you at once. It is not an agreeable thing to say to a lady, but still it must be said."

"Would Mr. Roggmoore say it?" Flora asked?"

Decidedly he would. He had come there purposely to say it, and it was this— he would not submit to interference in his affairs at the hands of any person, not even at the hands of an angelic being like Miss Heartley, who was universally believed to be of some divine origin. He was himself a man of the earth, earthy; but he considered himself, notwithstanding, more eminently qualified to conduct his own private business, whether in love or law, than any other individual in the universe, either man, woman, or angel, to which last class Miss Heartley was supposed to belong.

Surprise, not indignation, sparkled in Flora's eyes at this singular address. "You speak riddles, Mr. Roggmoore! What have I done?"

"In plain, unvarnished terms, Miss Heartley, you have striven to set your friend, Miss Percy, against me, her affianced husband."

"No I have not."

"A bold denial, fair lady."

"Because a true one."

"I am credibly informed that only yesterday you used all your powers of persuasion to dissuade Margaret from accepting me."

"That is not true. I know nothing against you, Mr. Roggmoore. Why should I speak against you?"

"Well argued; but not unanswerable. Did not sweet Margaret condescend to tell you that she had accepted me, but that she detested me? And did you not tell her not to accept me?"

"No. I only said, 'Then why accept him?' It was a natural question."

"Most natural; but you had no business to ask it, fair Flora. It would be far better if you would confine yourself to your round of parochial duties as the Vicar's daughter, visit your old women, and carry broth and sermons to the sick, than come here propounding questions to Miss Percy."

"You are very vexed, Mr. Roggmoore, or you would not be so very rude."

"Thank you."

"No don't thank me. Perhaps I should be acting with more dignity if I left the room without replying to your severe speeches; but I won't. I believe you love Margaret, and I pity you."

"Dove-eyed pity," sneered Charles Roggmoore, "is not to my taste."

"Miss Percy has promised to be your

wife, Mr. Roggmoore, and I think I know Margaret well. You will never find her failing in one single duty. A good daughter will be a good wife."

"What a comforting reflection! But do you know, Miss Heartley, that cold duty is my abhorrence. I would have love—love uncontrolled, burning and devoted as my own—and of this you, and such as you, have striven to rob me."

"Oh no, no! I have not. I only tried to argue Miss Percy out of her disbelief in love, and its continuance. Now listen to me patiently, Mr. Roggmoore. Margaret loves no one else. Her nature is not really as cold and worldly as she would have you and me to imagine. Try honestly to obtain her love, try to deserve it, and it will be yours."

Flora's was the soft answer that turneth away wrath. Charles Roggmoore was now completely disarmed, and felt very much ashamed of his unmanly attack on one so good, gentle, and beautiful as Miss Heartley.

"Forgive me," he said. "You are really an angel, Miss Flora, and I am a brute; but I am maddened at Margaret's contempt. Are you sure she loves no one else?"

"I am positive."

"I will even infringe on that kindness which is so justly, so universally esteemed. Will you say a good word for me in Margaret's ear?"

"I will. I will tell her that I think she has no right to despise any man's honest love, and that such I verily believe yours to be."

Just for an instant a faint flush came into Mr. Roggmoore's cheek; but he said then, in a deep voice, "God knows, I never loved any one so well before."

He spoke truly, never before had he met with the slightest opposition in all the various pursuits and amours that he had undertaken. Never before had his fine person, polished manners, and well feigned affection failed in drawing forth a love of some kind from the objects of his attentions. Some, like Grace, had fallen victims to his rank and wealth; others, like Emma, had yielded themselves up, body and soul, to become the slaves of his will; and had worshipped the cold, calculating libertine with an idolatrous worship. Never before had one dared, like Margaret Percy, to give him scorn for his flattery, contempt for his devotion, hatred for his love; and so the novelty of the thing amazed him, and the fickle man of the world almost believed that he loved Margaret Percy truly.

"I will say good morning to you, Miss Heartley; but you do not ask me who it was that told me of your private conversation with Miss Percy? It was Gretchen, her German maid."

Gretchen was a pretty, plump, blue-eyed Austrian, who had lived with Miss Percy four years.

"I give up my authoress because I feel

that she strove to mislead me. I give you leave to tell Miss Percy, and to advise her to dismiss the eavesdropper."

"Strange that she should choose you for her confidante," Flora could not help saying.

"Strange! Not at all. You forget how long I have lived in Germany. Gretchen and I are old friends. I have lodged in her father's house."

"And now you counsel her dismissal. Oh, Mr. Roggmoore!"

"Well, well. But what right had the little stumpy German to set me against you?"

"I cannot imagine," and then Flora Heartley inclined her head, and went out of the room.

Charles Roggmoore's statement was false. Gretchen had years ago fallen a victim to his perfidy. A mere chance had afterwards placed her in the service of Miss Percy. Not aware of her betrayer's rank in the first place, poor Gretchen had long ago, when she had discovered that he was a gentleman, given up all hopes of his righting her, but she loved him still, with a blind, unquestioning, humble devotion. She guarded his secrets, and looked after his interests. She knew that he wished to marry Miss Percy, and having been a concealed witness of the conversation between the two girls, her imperfect knowledge of English led her to imagine that Miss Heartley was warning Miss Percy against Mr. Roggmoore. On his part he would not have regretted the dismissal of his victim in the least. But in this hope he was disappointed. Flora breathed no word of the conference between herself and Charles Roggmoore to Margaret. She was too good and too wise for this, and all that day, and the next, things went smoothly as a marriage bell at Percy Priory, but on the third day from that on which Paul had warned his sister that he would only give her a week, during which she was to come to some definite arrangement with Charles Bingham Roggmoore, Charles Roggmoore rode into the pathway leading to Roggmoore Lodge.

It was an autumn evening, wild and wet; the mist hung in wreaths over the mountains and thickened the obscurity of the valleys, the damp leaves clogged the pathway, the wind moaned heavily; nature seemed to weep and wail and deck herself in palls of cloud and vapour.

Charles Roggmore hallooed loudly to the groom, but no one came. The rain fell steadily, but neither voice nor footstep echoed from the house, which appeared perfectly deserted. Cursing in no measured terms the whole of the household, Mr. Roggmore descended from his horse, and was about to lead him himself to the stable, when the back door opened suddenly and Emma came out in the rain—her hair was disordered, she wore a thin dress of light muslin. Her face was strangely pale.

"Charles, go in, I'll lead your horse round and unsaddle him," and he walked in.

" Where's John ?"

" Out."

" And Martin ?"

" Out too."

" And that rascal of a Louis ?"

" Out.   All gone into Aberglace."

He gave a short scornful laugh.   " You may lead my horse round to the stable since you choose to let those rascals go out."

And the delicate woman in her thin, fragile dress, led the horse round to the stable through the soaking rain, herself unsaddled him and placed corn in his reach; then she returned to the house wet through, her hair dishevelled, her garments shrunk.

By a fire in the dining room she found Charles Roggmoore, who had drawn off his boots, thrust his feet into slippers, and was lolling in an arm chair.

" Have you something for my dinner ?" he asked moodily, and without taking his eyes from the fire.

" Yes, plenty of everything."

" Serve it up then, please, I'm hungry."

She laid the cloth herself and brought up a tongue, fowls, a pasty, a silver jug frothing with ale.

He looked up astonished; "Where are the maids?"

"Out."

"And your mother?"

"Out also, you and I are alone in the house."

"The devil!" he exclaimed. "Whose pretty contrivance is this?"

"Mine. I received the letter stating that you were coming to-day, intended for my mother; I burnt it, and wrote another as though from you, telling her to go to Aberdare to nurse you, as you were taken ill there. She went off to-day at two o'clock. Aberdare is too far off for me to dread her return until to-morrow. I gave all the servants leave to stay in Aberglace until to-morrow. Albert went to London yesterday; we are safe from interruption."

Charles Bingham Roggmoore's answer was not long to this piece of information, but it was emphatic. He stood up, set his teeth hard, looked Emma in the face, and then said very much as if he meant it—"damn you!"

She turned very white, and put up her hand, as though she dreaded that the curse might be followed by a blow.

"Charles, you have been cruel, cruel cruel." She shrieked out each word louder than the other. "You have avoided me, neglected me, kept out of my way. If I had not devised this plan to speak to you alone, I could never have spoken at all, and I will speak. I will, I will," and she burst into a tempest of sobs and cries. "Did you not strive for my love? Did you not woo me in your false sweet voice? Did you not educate me? flatter me? mislead me? Did you not come like the sun to make a bright place in my dark poverty stricken life, with your false shine? Ah! can you give me back the young warm heart, which was all yours, and which you now despise? You cannot, Charles Roggmoore. You have desolated my whole existence.

"Then if I can do nothing, madam, why all this tearing and howling?"

"Because," said Emma, breaking, on her part, into passion at his disdain; "because, though you seem to have ceased to love me, you shall do me justice. I will be righted, if I die the next instant."

He laughed cruelly. "Do your worst. Begin at once; but be kind enough to state what you consider to be doing you justice What do you expect?"

"Need you ask?"

"Oh, no! I can pretty well guess. But now, once for all, and just to put your mad ideas to flight, listen to me. Do you suppose that when Wylde, the artist, more than five years ago, recommended your mother to me as housekeeper, at which time I was a youth of one-and-twenty; do you suppose that he and she had not laid their heads together? Ah! you wince. What were you brought here for, if not for a trap to ensnare me? The bait was laid, and took pretty well. At first I fancied the housekeeper's daughter was a non-such, and the housekeeper's daughter chose to fancy that I was a hero or a demi-god, and she worshipped me accordingly. She was not over burdened with maidenly reserve, was the housekeeper's daughter. The very proper restraint which is exercised abroad, where young women are concerned, was not practised here. The mother would leave the daughter alone for hours with me, a young man of pleasure and of the world. The sweet flower was not too shy. She wept at my departure, and welcomed me on my arrival, with an absence of reticence that went far towards extinguishing my affection in the bud. I like modest women.'

"Wretch! Perjured villain!" Emma burst out furiously. "Do you dare to insult, to taunt me, your own wedded wife? Yes, I will proclaim my position to-morrow from the house-tops. You shall not ride over to Percy Priory to court Cecil

Percy's white-faced daughter under my very eyes. I will go to her this night, and tell her all."

"By God," he answered, and he turned livid round the mouth, "if you do, I'll murder you."

"Hah! Charles Roggmoore, you have done worse. You have broken my heart."

"Oh, confound your heart," he interrupted, brutally. "You were never anything but a man-trap laid to ensnare me. Do you dare to stand before me, *you, you,* and call yourself the wife of a Roggmoore, of Roggmoore? Listen to me, woman. I abhor, I detest you. And now, go take poison, or anything else you like."

A change passed over Emma's face at those words. A strong expression, rigid, but the reverse of calm, settled upon her features. She put her hand to her heart, as though to ascertain if its pulses had not ceased. She went up to the table, and held it, as if to save herself from falling. Then she spoke.

"Charles, you have altered my whole inward being by those words. I will go away. You shall never be troubled by me again in person, but—" and she held up her finger, "remember, I am your wife before Heaven, and in the sight of men, and I will proclaim it to the world."

"My wife! Is the girl mad? because I took you into a Catholic Chapel in London? We both being Protestants, such a marriage is not legal."

"Do you remember how eager you were for the marriage, Charles Roggmoore? and how we stole away from Severntown, where I had gone on a visit to some recent acquaintance? How they believed me to be here while I was all the time with you in London, and there we passed a fortnight? Then you used to tell me of the time when you would acknowledge me to the world. You talked to me of all things beautiful in your wicked, dulcet voice. You taught me, you praised me, you deceived me."

"And most willingly were you deceived.

Now then, listen to me again. I am sorry for my impatience just now. I am sorry that I forgot what was due to you as a woman, to myself as a gentleman and a Roggmoore. Will you grant me your attention for a moment?"

"I am listening," said Emma, coldly.

"Very well. You are not legally my wife. At the same time, if you choose to go about and bruit this foolish story of the Catholic priest you may do me much mischief. Your own character also will suffer. At present it is unsuspected, even in that hive of hornets, Aberglace. Now I propose to settle three hundred a year on you for life. I will do it through my London lawyer. You and your mother will then go to a distant part, where you may live unmolested, and where you will soon marry well. Do you agree to this?"

"No," said Emma, coldly. "No. You, who have taught me languages, music, painting; you, who have impressed me with a love of the elegancies of life—I was going to say with a love of the beautiful, but that would not be true, for all that is good is beautiful, and you have taught me nothing good. But you, who have made me a lady; you, who taught me life's conventionalities; you, whom I have long regarded as the bravest and noblest of men, I now despise. Yes, Charles Bingham Roggmoore, of Roggmoore, I despise you; but, oh! I love you still. While life lasts, so will love; but I will none of your gold."

"What the devil will you have, then?" he broke out, testily. You are not my wife. Any lawyer will prove that to you in five minutes; and if you love me, as you profess to do, you can't mean to carry the tale of the mock marriage about, can you?"

Emma smiled bitterly. "The poor wretch whom you detest, abhor, and trample on, Charles Roggmoore, is yet free. I keep my own counsel. I tell none of my intentions. Good bye." And before he could stay her she had left the room.

He went out into the passage and cried aloud to her; but the howling wind and the driving rain were the only sounds that answered him. He then took a light and searched the whole house; but emptiness and void were all that greeted him. Emma had fled into the wild night. Then the man, *comme il faut*, returned to his meal. He heaped more logs on the fire; and when he had supped he threw himself luxuriously amid the pillows of the velvet couch, and smoked a delicious cheroot with a smiling face. He was making up a tale to tell the Percy's in case Emma should go there with her story. So the night wore away, and the fourth day of Paul's week shone over the mountains. Mr. Roggmoore soon arose and went to his room, where he washed, changed his clothes, and put on another riding coat. Then he descended to the stable, saddled his horse, mounted him, and then rode once more towards Percy Priory. Two hours' sharp riding brought him there. The household were already astir, and nothing unusual appeared to have happened. He was told, however, that Miss Percy was rather indisposed, and would breakfast in her own room. Mr. Percy would be down in a few moments. He was then shewn into the breakfast parlour, where a bright fire, rendered necessary by the sharpness of the autumnal morning, seemed to welcome him. Presently Cecil Percy entered the room. His greeting was frank and cordial. He had heard nothing.

"You are back again soon, Charles."

"Yes. Some mad hoax that my housekeeper's mad daughter has played upon us all. She actually sent off her mother and all the servants yesterday, so that I was quite alone in the house, with no one to light a fire or get me a cup of tea; so I am come back a pensioner on your bounty."

Mr. Percy smiled slightly, the mad freak of the housekeeper's daughter did not appear to have any interest for him; indeed the actions of people in that rank seldom elicited any attention from him at all. He talked about parliamentary matters, while the powdered lacqueys served up the recherché breakfast.

Presently another footman came in. "A young person to see Miss Percy, and as Miss Percy was ill she would like to see Mr. Percy."

Charles Bingham sat perfectly collected, throwing crusts of buttered roll to Miss Percy's favourite Italian greyhound. He even smiled when the footman dwelt on the pertinacity of the young person and her refusal to go away.

Mr. Percy looked annoyed. "Tell the person to send in her message."

"She refuses, Sir."

"Well, show her into the cloak room, and tell her I am at breakfast."

Up glanced the man of the world with a cold smile on his moustached lip. "Better have her in here. I know what she will say. She's mad."

"Shew her in, then," said Mr. Percy; and she was shewn in. Bonnetless, with her

garments soiled and torn, her hair hanging
in wild disorder round her white face, the
expression of which was fearful in its suffering agony, stood Emma Withers opposite
to her betrayer, in the great man's carpeted
saloon. *He*, meanwhile, threw another
buttered crust to the lap-dog, and smiled
carelessly.

Emma was struck speechless at the un-
expected sight of the cruel man she loved.
She could do nothing but stare hopelessly
from him to Mr. Percy. Fatigue and
hunger had done their work upon her, and
her courage failed her at the last.

"What do you wish to say to me, young
woman?" asked Mr. Percy.

But Emma did not speak. Her lips
moved, and she caught at the back of a
polished oak chair for support. Charles
Roggmoore flourished his silk handkerchief
round the head of the lap dog, and made
him jump after the end of it. He took no
notice whatever of Emma. His unconcern
frightened her, but the next moment it

inspired her with that courage which springs from rage. She walked right up to the fire-place, and stood between the two gentlemen.

"Sir, is that man about to marry your daughter?"

Mr. Percy was too indignant to reply, so Emma spoke again.

"He cannot marry your daughter, because I am already his wedded wife."

Charles Roggmoore laughed a low soft laugh, and flung his handkerchief over the dog's eyes.

"Do you hear what she says, Fan, Fan? She says she's my wife. What a great naughty fib. Isn't it then, Fan, Fan?"

"Liar!" shrieked Emma. "Liar! I am your wife. You married me in London, and you shall not marry this old dotard's daughter until I have told him, and her also, that they are walking straight to perdition if they suffer your addresses."

"This person is surely not fit to be at large," said Mr. Percy to Charles Bingham.

"What have you been about, my dear Charles, to bring yourself into the power of a person of this kind?"

"Nothing at all," said the other, looking up frankly. I assure you I am quite at a loss to understand the good girl's ravings, but," he added, significantly touching his forehead, "it is all easily explained."

"Do you dare insinuate I am mad? Do you dare deny that?—"

"There, there," said Charles Roggmoore, smoothly, "it's all right. Don't make a fuss. It is no use to rave and tear in other people's houses. Pray go away. I will see to all this again."

"Again," said Emma. "Again. What can you do? What would you do if I went away? But I will not go away. I am your wife, and will not be trampled on, and turned out, that you may pay court to this man's icy daughter."

"Produce your proof, if you are my wife," said Mr. Roggmoore, coolly. "Produce your witnesses."

"You have the proof, you have the paper," said Emma, sobbing. "You know I can prove nothing."

"Then walk out of my house," said Mr. Percy, rising from his chair, and pointing to the door. "If you come here again I will give you to the police."

She stopped in her rapid walk across the room, and said, "Will you? What do you say to my knowing the whole story of the Northumberland village? Yes, and the *torn leaf?*"

Charles Bingham Roggmoore, Esq., was at first impressed with the idea that Emma had lost her senses in reality; but the effect on Mr. Percy was almost miraculous. He made one step forward, and then fell down heavily on the floor in a fit. They raised him up, and loosened his cravat, but life appeared extinct. Emma rushed away when she had produced this wonderful effect. A fleet horse was saddled, and a groom despatched at full speed to Aberglace, to summon Paul Withers at once to Percy Priory.

The proud man lay like a senseless log
on the velvet sofa of the breakfast room.
Charles Bingham bent anxiously over him.

" The torn leaf," he muttered to himself.
" What can the mad fool have meant ?"

Then Margaret came flying into the room.
She really loved her father, and in eager
accents gave orders that he should instantly
be placed in a hot bath.   Mr. Withers had
said that a hot bath was the safest remedy
for a fit.   He was placed in one, and then
in his bed.   He opened his eyes, and gave
some signs of returning life.

In about four hours time from the departure of the groom, Paul, splashed with
mud, and heated from his rough and hasty
ride, came into the sick man's room.   He
bled him a little, and the patient fainted.
On his recovery, Paul asked for the me-
dicine chest, and himself compounded
a draught, to be taken every three hours.
All this time, Margaret, to whom he had
only slightly bowed on entering, had scarcely
once taken her eyes from his face, and now

she came forward as he was leaving the room, and signed to him to follow her into a small sitting room on the same floor.

"Will my father live, Mr. Withers?" She went up close to him, and caught his arm in both of her hands. "He is the only being on whose love I have any claim. Oh, say that he will not die?"

The beautiful face, usually so pale in its still repose, was now slightly flushed with excitement. The hair was disordered, the eyes unwontedly bright. Paul gazed upon her beauty, and forgot to frame a fitting reply. His lips moved, and still Margaret clasped his arm, as though he were her friend, and looked up into his flushed and happy face, and just at this instant the door burst open, and Charles Bingham Roggmoore entered.

Paul was, of course, alive to their awkward position, but Miss Percy, utterly unconscious of any feeling but anxiety for her father's life, and friendly reliance on Paul, did not attempt to disengage her hold of his arm, and only darted a look of careless dislike towards her affianced husband. Mr. Roggmoore was quite off his guard, and a thrill of jealous rage possessed him.

"I am scarcely wanted here, Miss Percy," he said bitterly.

Margaret awoke to a sense of her position, blushed, and let go her hold of Paul's arm, but then, turning to Mr. Roggmoore, she said, haughtily, "What do you mean?"

"I mean," he answered angrily, and forgetting for once his usual sneer, "that I am astonished to find Miss Percy *tete à tete* with the doctor's man."

"This is the doctor himself," said Margaret, quietly, "on whose skill depends my dear father's life. I choose to be *tete a tete* with him, and if it surprises you, I cannot help that."

"I am to understand, then, that I am not wanted here."

"Understand any thing you like," said Margaret, beginning to weep. "Why will you come tormenting me with your airs and follies, while life and death are struggling for the mastery in the next room?"

Paul looked from one to the other, and his old antagonistic feelings towards the polished man returned in full force. By this time Mr. Roggmoore had recovered his temper, and wishing to efface the remembrance of his rude words from Paul's mind, he took Miss Percy's hand, saying, "Come, Margaret, I wonder whether you will be as anxious about me, if I should be ill, after we are married?"

"Married! good Heaven! Then this smooth-cheeked villain was to win Margaret and Emma?" Paul almost staggered towards the door. The week that he had promised to maintain silence had not expired; but what of that? Then again, was it not absurd of him to fancy for one moment that this gentleman would ever have married his sister? It was not to be thought of, and Emma had again and again declared that she had met with no wrong at his hands. After all, it was perhaps but a foolish flirtation. But Emma really and truly loved this man. He had blighted her happiness, if he had done no worse; and Paul felt that he hated him, independent of his being the winner of Margaret, that pearl of great price, so far removed from his own reach. What with his love, and his sister's wrongs, his own pathway seemed sufficiently darkened. One great overmastering affection for any human being, one thought for ever and for ever possessing complete sway, and bending the whole of the faculties subservient to its will. One tyrant, hopeless passion, scorching, with the breath of that fire that is kindled by unrequited love, is of itself a trial sufficient to pale the cheek of youth, and sometimes to sadden a lifetime. Paul suffered all this. His was no tame, calculating nature, as his sister imagined. He loved desperately. To him existence had lost its charm. He was only twenty-three; but he had ceased to think life sweet.

Already had " crazy sorrow " asserted her
empire, and Paul had truly (or untruly)
longed for death more than once. But he
wished to pay his debt to Reginald; he
wished to see his sister righted. There
were times when he even had some of his
old longings for fame and wealth; but
through all these dreams there shone the
pure, passionless face of his high born
love.

Poor Paul! He returned to his post, by
Mr. Percy's bed, and there he remained all
day. Margaret, too, was there, and Paul
almost looked his passion through his eyes
whenever he gazed upon her. *She* was
only filled with the thought of her father.

Mr. Roggmoore was walking up and
down a secluded part of the shrubbery,
where the damp leaves lay in heaps, and
while the wind sighed sadly through the
branches. He wore no hat, and his fair
uncovered hair was straying almost wildly
over his brows. In his hand he held a
torn sheet of vellum, old and yellow, and

faded; but the characters traced thereon were sufficiently legible. A glow was on his cheek, and a peculiar smile on his lip, and he muttered to himself, " *Par Dieu!* a good weapon to hold over the proud vixen, Margaret. Oh how delicious to present her with this paper, and coolly assure her that her father's possessions, and great name even, are all a delusion and a lie. What a blessing to humble that little devil. I will do it too, by George! but afterwards, of course, I will destroy the torn sheet. First, though, I will bend that stubborn head, and make her sue to me for mercy on her father. Hah!" He came to a stand-still, for a step sounded behind him. He turned, and there stood an elderly lady, dressed in black silk. Her white hair was arranged smoothly under her black satin bonnet. A large grey shawl was wrapped not ungracefully round her figure. She was sallow, with great dark eyes, and regular features. Our readers have seen her before, one wet evening in the spring, at her own dull home, "Bithol," presiding over the muffins and a tea-urn; but Charles Roggmoore had never seen her before. "Hah!" said he, crumpling the leaf in his hand and thrusting it into his breast pocket.

Madame Williams's cheek glowed a little at the sight of the torn sheet, and she exclaimed involuntarily, "You have found it!"

Charles Roggmoore crossed his arms over his chest, and bowed to Madame Williams.

In that one moment the woman saw the object of years of patient waiting, earnest striving, plotting, and counterplotting, placed beyond her reach. It required an almost superhuman effort to appear calm under the circumstances; but Madame Williams contrived to do so.

"You know what I conceal here," said Charles Roggmoore, touching his chest.

"Je sais, et je ne sais pas," said Madame Williams, promptly. "A wild girl, whom I fear you have rather misled, Mr. Roggmoore, has been talking nonsense about a torn sheet I know not what. I come to you on her part."

"I am all attention," said Mr. Roggmoore."

"I come to propose that you grant her an interview at my house, where she is now staying. I have long taken an interest in Emma Withers. Will you honour my poor house with your presence this evening? I assure you you will find it to your advantage to conciliate that very excitable young person. You may be a great gentleman; but still, even a great gentleman should try and stand fair with the world."

"My gratitude should be boundless, madame, for the interest you manifest in my unworthy self."

"I can dispense with compliments, even from you, Mr. Roggmoore. I have had my share of them in my time. I want no more."

"Then perhaps, madame, you will allow

me to wish you good evening, and to return to the house. The air is chilly."

Madame Williams made one more effort. She laid her hand on Mr. Roggmoore's shoulder. "You will come to me this night I feel convinced. Grant poor Emma one more interview, else she may seriously annoy you."

Charles Bingham moved away from the clasp of the thin brown hand.

"Whom have I the honour of addressing, madame?"

"Sir, I am the holder of a small freehold purchased from Mr. Percy. Williams is my name, and I live at Bithol."

"Indeed. I have heard the name. And so you are particularly anxious that I should visit your charming retreat? Perhaps some time between this and next summer I may do myself that honour. But will you not walk into the house, madame, and take some slight refreshment?"

"I need none at all. But pray do not

put me off in this way. I am anxious for poor Emma."

"I cannot possibly excite my nerves by another interview with that very demonstrative person this evening, madame. Perhaps I may call to-morrow," and Charles Roggmoore bowed, and walked off, with the torn sheet of vellum safely buttoned under his waistcoat.

Madame Williams remained standing under the yellow branches of the trees. When he was out of sight, she fastened her hands together, clenched her teeth, and rocked her head backwards and forwards. At last she spoke. She raised her hand and shook it menacingly in the direction of the Percy's lordly house.

"If I have to take life, if I have to wade through blood to obtain it, I will possess myself of that torn leaf. I will cast Cecil Percy from his house. His house? It is not his. The rightful owner shall step into it. The true heir shall sit down on its soft cushioned chairs, shall lie on its downy beds, shall drink from its golden goblets, shall spurn with his heel its velvet carpets. But down passion. I must be calm. I must act like a machine. Thank Heaven, I can act," and Madame Williams went round by a back way to the road, where she found her little pony and phæton awaiting her. She stepped into it, and drove off.

Meanwhile, Mr. Roggmoore returned to the house. By the fire, in the dining room, he partook of a meal that was served up to him. Nobody came near him. He finished his dinner hastily, then lighted a lamp, and sat down, apparently to read a paper, but in reality to ruminate.

This was how he had found the torn sheet. When Margaret had followed Paul into the sick room of her father, Mr. Roggmoore had turned into the portrait gallery, and taken some hasty strides up and down to compose his feelings. There he had suddenly come to a stand before a painting of a certain Lady Dacette, a daughter of the Percy family. He paused there, because

Margaret was supposed to have some resemblance to this great aunt, who was painted in the unbecoming short-waisted dress of the last century, but whose sweet pale face beamed still in beauty from the canvas.

"It is a far gentler face than Margaret's," was his thought, "and yet I like Margaret's style better."

He stopped a moment, and was then about to walk away, when his foot caught in the claws of a little old fashioned, richly carved cabinet, which had stood always within his memory exactly where it stood now.

It was a curiously contrived article. Many of the miracles were carved upon it, and the figures were as large as children's usual sized dolls, that is to say, a foot high. Now in falling, Charles Roggmoore caught at the figure of St. Peter, who was walking carefully through some dark coloured waves. St. Peter came off in his hands, and Charles Roggmoore scrambled up again. St. Peter was not broken. The figures were placed in sockets, and Charles Roggmoore had wrenched this one out. He was going to put it in again, when he saw something like a leaf of vellum rolled up in the cavity. He pulled it out, opened it, and then rushed with it to the room which he usually occupied at Percy Priory. Some hours later we find him in the shrubbery, still perusing the same startling sheet of vellum.

"This is true, and plain, and positive," he muttered to himself, as he sat by the lamp light. "What a strange caprice of fate. Doubtless that paper has been concealed there for years. What would not Cecil Percy give to be possessed of it? What can Emma know about it? Ah!" He looked up, for he heard a step, and there stood Emma, still with the fearful agonised face she had worn in the morning, still bonnetless, still drenched with rain, still trembling.

"Charles." He rose, and stirred the fire.

"I came in the back way."

"Did you?"

"Charles, have mercy on me. Do you know that if I live"—she came closer to him and whispered some words in his ear.

"Can I help that," he said coldly. "Did I not offer last night to make a suitable provision for you? Unless you leave me in peace I will make no provision at all. A fine tale you have made of yourself by this time. Do you not think that all the cackling women at Aberglace are making merry with your story? Shame on you. Where is your pride?"

"It all went last night, Charles, when you used those dreadful words, 'Woman, I detest you, I abhor you; now go and take poison, or anything else you like.' I keep saying those words over to myself every moment."

"More fool you; I spoke them in passion."

"Did you! oh, say that again, Charles! I love you, still love you with my whole heart. Oh, have pity upon me! Say you

are not about to marry Miss Percy! Forgive me!"

She knelt to him, anxious for one word of
love—false love even if he would grant it
to her—he did not give it.

"How did you come here?"

"I walked."

"How will you get back?"

"Walk again."

"Where will you go?"

"To Bithol."

"Do you want any money?"

"None. One word of kindnes rather.
Tell me you have some pity for me—some
sorrow for the deceit you practised. Tell
me that for our unborn child you have some
love."

A step sounded on the thick carpet, the
firm, heavy tread of a strong man. Paul
had been sent down to dine in this very
room. At the half open door he had heard
the loud words of his excited sister. He
knew now the full extent of the wrong she
had suffered at the hands of Mr. Rogg-

moore. He advanced like a lion on his prey, doubled his fist, and dealt one savage blow on the sneering mouth of Charles Bingham Roggmoore—a well-aimed blow, which covered the face of the gentleman with blood, knocked out his front teeth, and stretched him half senseless on the floor. Paul glared over him with teeth and hands clenched; but spoke no word, his heart was beating too fast, and his tongue clove to the roof of his mouth. Charles Roggmoore rose slowly from the carpet. Emma did not shriek—her instincts told her that Mr. Roggmoore wanted no witnesses, but she clung passionately to him weeping and sobbing. He flung her rudely off, and then turned round upon Paul, and asked sharply, "Who are you?"

With white, parted lips, and eyes bright with rage, Paul stood and faced his foe; but in vain did he struggle for utterance, the depth of his feelings had for the time deprived him of the power of speech.

"Who are you?" repeated Charles Bing-ham. "Speak, low ruffian."

"I am Paul Withers, the brother of the lost, sin-stained creature you have blasted. I am Paul Withers, the surgeon, to whom you gave a fee in Burdett Court, in the New Cut, when Grace, a girl whom you had reduced to the lowest depth of infamy, was dying before your eyes. God forgive me for I thirst for your life blood. I will yet be avenged, and deeply too. Hell even shall not shield you from my fury."

Timmins, the butler, had been listening at the door, and he now rushed in and tried to collar Paul, who flung him off as he would have done a weed. Timmins was a time-server, and had a very great respect for Mr. Roggmoore's position.

"You heard this madman's threat, Tim-mins. It is not safe that he should be at large."

Paul went close up to Mr. Roggmoore, who put himself on the defensive.

"Not again, not here," said Paul, scornfully; "not in a pampered drawing room, within call of menials; but yet again, Charles Roggmoore, yet once again, we two men shall meet with no human witnesses to our deadly fight. God's sky shall be our covering, some lonely spot on God's earth shall be our trysting place, and there I will have eye for eye and tooth for tooth;" and then Paul, frenzied, rushed out of the room. Once he turned, and cast a look upon his sister Emma. She was clinging about her betrayer's knees in abject love and grovelling tenderness, the reaction after her haughty anger of the day before, and again and again he spurned her. He was in dreadful pain from the effect of Paul's blow, and, of course, was doubly irritated.

"Begone, she-devil; henceforth I disown you for ever; you and your murderous brother begone;" and the polished gentleman extricated himself from her embrace, and Timmins approached to thrust her from the door.

At that last indignity she rose and fled

towards Paul, who had opened the hall
door and stood on the step. He opened
his arms and she ran into them, and rested
her cheek on his shoulder, and looked into
his deathly pale face, rendered yet more
ghastly by the sickly beams of the autumn
moon. Neither spoke; but in that moment
of concentrated passion, the brother and
sister grew more into each other's hearts
than they had ever done before. Each was
leaving the object of youth's first adoration
within the stately walls of the house from
which they were thus expelled. On each
of them had fallen a lifelong sorrow, the
dark shadows of which stretched before
them, so they thought, even to the very
gates of eternity. One had sinned through
love; the other had sinned through hatred.
On one had a heavy punishment fallen; for
the other—the brave, ardent, honest Paul—
alas! for the "world's verdict" on his conduct. How is it that on some a darkness
and a great sorrow comes in the time of
youth?—how is it that there are many to

be found whose childhood has been as the
very gall of bitterness?   "Give me back,
give me back, that first freshness of morning; its smiles and its tears are worth evening's best light." Alas! for those over whom
the clouds have gathered darkly in the
morning, and who can only look back to
their youth through the mists of sad tears,
the weepings, and the mournings, and the
fastings, which follow in the train of poverty, and sickness, and shame.   The brother and sister went out of the Percy lands
hand in hand, and then out upon the mountain road with the night sky over them—
they clung together, and wept such tears as
angels might have pitied.   Paul spoke no
single word of reproach to his sister, he
only shielded her defenceless head with his
strong arm, and murmured words of love
and pity.

"We will go away, my Emma, far away
from this country.   We will return to London, and I will work hard at my profession,
and support you and my mother too.   The

little ones will come home in their holidays, and cheer us up, and we shall be contented, and some time or other we shall get rich."

"But, Paul, there is an unborn child, whose only heritage will be shame, and yet Heaven knows I believed I was his wife."

"What?"

"I believed I was his wife." And then Emma told Paul the tale of her marriage in a Catholic church, and how that Charles Roggmoore had told her that any lawyer would prove to her, in five minutes, that the marriage was invalid."

"It will admit of a question, and shall be contested," said Paul; but the next moment the deep consciousness of his poverty weighed heavily upon him, and he sighed aloud.

"And now, where are we to go, Emma? for to-night you are, indeed, weak and weary. Doctor Milton's horse is in the stables at Percy Priory, but I will not enter those grounds again while that villain is there. You shall never enter Roggmoore

Lodge again either. I have it. We must go to Bïthol. That strange woman told me to come to her in any trouble. Here is the trouble come indeed."

"Then you know Madame Williams, Paul?"

"A little. Do you?"

"As I know darkness and night, and tempest and sorrow. I know enough of her to shudder at the thought of her. It was last summer that I first made her acquaintance; last summer, when I was happy, walking along the road, gathering dog-roses, filled with the glad thought of my love, believing myself a wedded wife, with the bright sun shining over the corn fields, and my own heart leaping with joy. I went singing along, when Madame Williams and her pony phæton came to a stand before me. 'You seem merry, young lady.' I told her I felt so. 'Long may it continue,' she said, as though she wished for it to come to an end. 'Love makes the happiness of youth,' she said. 'It does,' I said.

'It is too often but a delusion and a snare,' she said, and she went on talking like a witch, and hinting of evils to come. She reminded me of Edgar Poe's raven in human form :—

> " 'Prophet,' said I. 'Thing of evil;
> " Prophet still, if bird or devil !
> " Take thy beak from out my heart,
> " And take thy form from off my door.'
> " Said the raven, ' Nevermore.' "

And truly, ever since then, I have never known but evil. Afterwards, this strange woman invited me to tea, and worried my secret out of me, that I loved Mr. Roggmoore, and she roused my jealousy terribly by hinting that Mr. Percy wanted him for his daughter, and the other night, when I left Roggmoore Lodge, I ran straight to Bithol, 14 miles through the night, and poured my troubles into her ear. Then she told me to go to Percy Priory and expose Charles. She told me that if I could manage to get into the picture gallery, and there search for and find a certain torn sheet of parchment, hidden, she believed, in the wainscotting, or behind the pictures, she would make my fortune, and prevent Mr. Roggmoore from marrying Miss Percy. She said she had been for years trying to find that torn leaf, and that only last week, a part of an old letter had been sent her, which said, 'The leaf I have hidden in the portrait gallery in ——, and there the paper was torn, and as there were several houses in the Percy family, and in each a portrait gallery, she could not be sure of her object. She impressed upon me that I was not to lose my self-command, but this, you know, I did most wofully, and never thought of the torn sheet until old Percy insulted me, and then, as I supposed he did not wish to have the torn sheet found, I said, in a passion, that I had found it, and he fell immediately into a fit."

"Wonderful," said Paul. "There is deep mystery here." And he pondered in silence over Emma's recital until they arrived at Bïthol, which stood about two miles from Percy Priory. It looked even more gloomy to Paul in the autumn moonlight with the mountains, which already looked dark as with the foreboding of winter storms standing frowning around it, than it had looked in the spring storm of six months back. He knocked at the door.

Emma shuddered, and clung to his arm. "It is like a sepulchre, this house," she said.

Old Sarah opened the door.

"Is Madame Williams in?" asked Paul.

"No. She's drove into Aberglace. She'll be back to-night. Are you the doctor?"

"Yes."

"Walk in." And she ushered them into the parlour, and lighted a lamp. There was no fire in the room.

Emma shivered. "I am perished with cold," she said.

"How can you tell your mistress will be back to-night?" asked Paul. "It's thirty-six miles from here to Aberglace and back."

"She'll be back afore morning, however,"

said old Sarah. "She left word as any time you came you was to be made welcome. Will you have tea?"

"Yes, please," said Emma; "and, oh! do light a fire."

"You'll not be feeling well, I warrant," said old Sarah, coarsely. "You've been a great fool—that just what you've been."

Paul thought that of all the repulsive women he had ever met with old Sarah was the most repulsive.

She lighted a fire and made Emma a cup of tea, and all the time she talked incessantly, pitilessly. "I've seed many a girl a going wrong, and a believing alls the chaps tells 'em, and I always says to 'em 'You're great fools, that's what *you* are;' and so you are. What do you suppose now yon feller cares for you? He wouldn't care if you was dead to-morrow—not he."

While the amiable Sarah was making these refined observations she was thrusting sticks into the fire, and occasionally blowing it with the bellows. She never once looked at her auditors, whom she firmly believed to be in the humble enjoyment of her sage remarks. I have once been in the house with the old Sarah of this story, for I knew her in the flesh when very great darkness and sorrow had fallen upon the family in which she resided. At that time none of us were able to extract the ludicrous from her conversation, and to amuse ourselves therewith we were too wretched; and so we had to sit and listen patiently while the privileged old servant, with the thin evil face and harsh croaking voice, dug deep into our wounded feelings with her yellow claws, and insulted us all round to our heart's content. The best of it was, old Sarah never looked at you while she went on talking. She interrupted you if you dared to speak, and, with a coarse unconscious brutality, raked up your sorrows (of which, unfortunately through circumstances, she knew too much) and riddled and sifted them through with her pitiless hands. If the writer of these pages has a

mortal antipathy it is for the identical old
Sarah of this story. Byron's much con-
demned address, commencing "Born in a
garret, in a kitchen bred," occurs to my
mind at this time. I feel very much towards old Sarah as he seems to have felt
towards the heroine of that celebrated piece.
It is just because the old lady is too deeply
steeped in ignorance to rise even to the
level of contempt that I abhor her. She
rose superior to any mollifying, any reasoning, by the sheer strength of an obtuse
perception and a brutal nature. "You are
a liar if you say that," I have heard her
observe to a remarkably truthful, somewhat
over-sensitive person, who was in the room
with her. "You're a liar if you say that—
and that's what you are." So she continued
to talk away while Emma sipped her tea,
and Paul, with his hand on his forehead,
paced up and down the room.

Presently came the welcome ring, which
announced Madame Williams, and in a few
moments that lady entered. "I have not

been to Aberglace," said she, taking off her bonnet and shawl and giving them to Sarah, and she added, "You need not return until I ring."

So Sarah decamped, and Paul and Emma mentally thanked Heaven.

"Mr. Withers," said Madame Williams, extending her hand to Paul. "I asked you to come to me when in trouble, and you have come."

"This is fearful trouble, madame. It calls for vengeance."

Madame Williams smiled, and took a chair. "Sit down, Mr. Withers."

"I cannot, madame. I am too much enraged to sit for an instant."

"Will you grant me then your complete attention?"

"Oh, yes."

"Your enemy has actually, I believe, though I haven't read it, found a parchment, on which depends an enormous, an overwhelming result. A parchment, which I have plotted to obtain for thirty-eight years. Get it from him, Paul Withers, and you shall see your sister righted. Your own fortune will be made. All shall be as bright as it is dark at present. Get that parchment from him before he destroys it. I have seen it, seen it in his hand to-day."

Her voice trembled with eagerness, and she laid her thin brown hand on Paul's shoulder, as she had laid it on Mr. Roggmoore's in the afternoon.

"How am I to get it from him, madame?"

"How? Have you not a strong arm? And is not the parchment buttoned under his waistcoat pocket? Is not your's a powerful fist? and have you not met with wrong at his hands?"

"He has felt the strength of my clenched fist already," said Paul, grimly, "but as for the parchment, I have no right to that."

"But I have. I tell you it is mine."

"But not mine," said Paul.

Madame Williams turned from him in scorn.

"You are but a weak fool after all," she said.

"I know it," said Paul, gloomily.

"Look here," said Madame Williams, again turning to him. "I have lived abroad, in all the cities where sojourned once the hider of that parchment, that I might try and trace it to its place, but all in vain. I have paid spies and searchers among the servants of the Percies, to try and bring this torn sheet to me, but all in vain. The first time I saw you, and heard you were the medical attendant of that man, I fancied that you might, in that capacity, worm the secret out of him, if ever he should be in danger of his life, and so learn whether *he* had ever found the parchment, for, of course, if he had, all my labour would have been spent uselessly. And now, now shall this torn sheet escape me? I swear, by all the saints, that it shall not."

"Why did you never before try to gain an entrance yourself into the house?"

"Because I was never sure that it was in

the house at all till last week. However, that is not the question. Will you tear that parchment from Mr. Roggmoore?"

"No, madame. One path I will follow. That which I honestly believe to be the right one. I will not deprive a man of what does not belong to me, any more than to him."

Madame Williams turned from Paul wrathfully. "What a very good young · man you are?" she exclaimed. "Your sister did me much harm when she flung out that threat to old Cecil Percy. Perhaps *she* will try and coax the parchment from Charles Roggmoore. Will you, Miss Emma?"

"I, madame. He detests, abhors me," and she buried her face in her hands.

"Well," said Madame Williams, "both of you young people seem singularly averse to assist *me*. Now, will you kindly state what you expect me to do for *you*?"

"Nothing more than to give my sister a bed for to-night, the price of which

I would not insult you by offering to pay."

"No," said Madame Williams, shortly interrupting him, "I don't keep an inn; but I will give your sister a bed."

"Then," said Paul, rising, "Will you name some other way in which I can oblige you? If not, I must find some means of shewing my gratitude."

"What a pretty speech; but sit down, Mr. Withers. I will give you a bed too."

"Not to-night, thank you. I cannot sleep, and I would far rather walk on to Aberglace. The eighteen miles walk over the mountains will do me good, and calm my nerves this fine night."

"And you downright refuse to get the paper from Charles Roggmoore?"

"Downright, madame; because I'm sure I should be doing wrong."

"Take a glass of ale or wine before you go? You look faint."

Paul did not refuse this courtesy. He

drank a glass of ale and ate a crust. Then embraced Emma and whispered words of comfort in her ear; and having wrung Madame Williams's hard, thin hand, he prepared to depart.

"You may long regret your refusal," said Madame Williams, as he was stepping out on the threshold. "Remember, young man, I stop at nothing. I sacrifice everybody to gain my object. Think of your revenge."

"Madam, I want no more than I have taken. Man has nothing to do with vengeance, and I even regret my wild words of mad rage, my terrible threats to Roggmoore. I would not harm him now if I could. To-morrow I shall be fined and summoned for an assault, I suppose. Anyhow, I intend to lay the case before Dr. Milton, and to leave Aberglace at once. I have a hundred good reasons now for wishing to return to London."

And Paul set out on his wild, beautiful moonlight walk. Sometimes, half spent

with the exertion, he would sit and rest under the boughs of some tall pine which
skirted the base of the mountain. Again
he would inhale the fragrant breath of the
heather, and feel refreshed, almost hopeful,
for a time. Deep trouble had come upon
him in the morning of his youth; but with
it all youth would not be utterly repressed.
He would go away. He would win fame,
riches, honour, in London—in the great
city where his boyish instincts had long ago
whispered to him that he must sojourn if he
wished to obtain wealth And Margaret?
Oh! why did he love her so fearfully?
She was to marry the man who had
wronged him. The pale, distant moon was
not further from him than she was, and her
blue, tender eyes had only that morning
looked tearfully into his, and her white,
fragile hands had clasped his arm. Good
God! what a frenzied, fearful thing is
love. How much of jealous rage had
nerved his arm when he had dealt that
terrible blow on Charles Roggmoore's fair

aristocratic face? He trembled to think; and he would never look again upon the delicate young face which had almost tempted him to sin. No, he would leave the mountains, amid which he had drunk so deeply of the sweet poison called passion. Henceforth he would possess his own soul in patience; he would be steadfast in right doing; he would pray. Yes, he would pray to the Dispenser of all good for strength and for blessing on his resolve.

The walk calmed his nerves, as he had foreseen, and he walked on firmly under the shadow of the night, thinking no evil. At one part of the road, where a rapid mountain stream crossed the path, he saw the figure of a man stooping beneath the weight of a bag. He accosted this person civilly. "Good night," said Paul. The person scarcely answered him; and, not being in a mood for conversation, he moved on. And the shadows of the night deepened, the moon dropped lower in the heavens, and then that " darkest hour which comes before the morning" shrouded the mountains and covered the valleys, and Paul walked on wearily in the blackness.

At last the grey morning shot feebly across the sky; then dimly, and as through a sad coloured mist, he began to discern the now familiar objects of the road. At last the " day beams from on high" came out vividly. A fresh breeze sprung up, and Paul now saw the glancing waters of the bay, tossing their white foam crests against the "cold grey stones" of the shore. Aberglace lay just at his feet, with its slate-coloured roofs shining in the sunshine, and the green still hills standing calmly around it. He looked across the wide, restless sea. Far towards the horizon's verge he sought for Pearl Island; but, though a sunny morning, the mists and white clouds lay low, and he could not discern that enchanted spot. He sat down at the edge of the hill top and buried his face in his hands. "How much of my inner self is changed

since I first came here a few short months
back. How much love has been 'spent'
on an unconscious, unthankful girl. How
much resolve and honest striving have been
thrown away uselessly. How has the cruel
tide of circumstance cast me back upon myself, wearied, worn, spiritless. No further
on in any one thing than when I started.
Disgraced, expelled, wretched. My heart
filled with a love, whic hmust, which will,
poison my whole existence. I have taken
the treasures of my affection and poured
them out at the feet of an unpitying idol.
I have no more capacity for loving. My
love is 'spent,' and I have received in
return a few soft words, a cold smile or
two—nothing more;" and large tears forced
their way through his entwined fingers, and
dropped on the grass silently. At last,
feeling this weakness unmanly, Paul arose
and walked erect in the direction of Aberglace. It was the fifth day of the week he
had given Emma—it was the sabbath. He
went straight to Doctor Milton's, where he

washed and dressed, and then sat down and sought solace in a commonplace, but never-failing comforter, a fragrant cigar, and he smoked until the stir in the house informed him that the doctor was awake and up; and he was not long in presenting himself to him in the breakfast room.

"Bless me, Mr. Withers, back so soon? I hope nothing has happened."

"Not to Mr. Percy. He was considerably better when I left last night."

"Last night!"

"Yes. I left at nine last night. I walked into Aberglace."

"What's the matter with the horse?"

"Nothing. I forgot to bring him."

"Mr. Withers, you are quite pale. Something has happened, I know. Tell me." And Doctor Milton got up and stood at the back of his chair, which he began to twirl uneasily about, and looked at Paul with a flushed, almost frightened face.

"Something has happened. I must leave Aberglace at once."

"The devil," said the doctor, testily. "What have you been about?"

"I knocked Charles Bingham Roggmoore, Esq., down and broke his front tooth."

"Good God! Mr. Withers, you must be raving mad to fight with the friends of my best patients. Mr. Roggmoore is to marry Miss Percy."

"I know it, Sir."

"Then, why *the deuce*," said Doctor Milton, losing his temper, "couldn't you keep your ruffianly hands off? You are no gentleman, Sir."

"Mr. Roggmoore is a gentleman," said Paul, speaking slowly. "He led my sister to believe that he had married her. He imposed upon her ignorance. He *did* marry her in a Catholic Church, and now he is to marry Miss Percy. Last night he mocked at her misery, and spurned her from him. I heard him, I saw him, and I knocked him down. His 'gentle blood' did not protect him one instant from my vengeance."

Doctor Milton let go of the chair and walked to the window, out of which he looked in silence, turning his back on Paul. "And what do you purpose doing?" he asked at length, coldly.

"Leaving Aberglace immediately."

"You may be summoned for an assault."

"Scarcely so. Mr. Roggmoore will hardly wish to make his villiany public."

"Then I scarcely see the necessity of your leaving if the affair is hushed up. You can apologise."

"I!" exclaimed Paul, loudly.

"Yes, certainly. It is usual in such cases."

"It would not be usual with men of honour to apologise for what they would do again under the like provocation."

"You acted very roughly, Sir; very brutally; very imprudently," said the doctor, walking up the room in a bustle. "You put me to great inconvenience. I must go myself to-day to Percy Priory. Your mother ought never to have let your sister live in the same house with those young men. Anybody might have foretold the issue. What a bore! What a confounded nuisance!"

Paul did not speak, but he looked at the unsympathising doctor with no friendly eyes.

" When is your quarter's salary due?" he asked Paul, sharply.

" The day after to-morrow."

" And you wish to leave then?"

" I do, Sir."

" Well, I tell you, I can't pay you before next month. You know how slowly people pay their debts in Aberglace."

" I can wait," said Paul.

Doctor Milton sat down again and sipped his coffee. "Have you had any break-fast?"

" Not yet."

" You'd better sit down and help your-self," said the doctor, who was beginning to regret his rude speeches.

And Paul, who did not much care for

the doctor one way or the other, sat down
and ate some toast and drank some coffee;
and then he resolved to go to church, and,
bidding the doctor a civil " good morning,"
he walked down the Parade, amid the
parti-coloured inhabitants of Aberglace, who
were shewing off the sheen of silks, and the
waving of feathers, and the draping of
shawls, to their hearts' content. The high
and mighty Mrs. Holt, who was a stout,
rosy woman of forty, rustled heavily on in
a puce brocade and a rich velvet mantle.
Her tall, slight daughter, a young effigy of
herself, went prancing gaily by her side in
a dress of cheaper material; and young
Hanway, of the Scotch Greys, who was
staying at the "Sea View," was talking in
loud familiar strain to mother and daughter,
as though somehow *he* didn't think them
high and mighty at all. "Johnnie," that
was the pet name of the younger Miss Holt,
who was not yet promoted to the full dignity of long dresses, and who wore a hat to
church, came running after the others, and

she appeared very thoroughly impressed with the idea that she was Miss Johnnie Holt, and of rather more importance than all the rest of Aberglace put together. Miss Johnnie was an heiress in a small way, and, though only fourteen, was quite aware of the advantages her grandmother's legacy gave her over her tall, portionless sister.

So the Holts went on and on, and entered the portals of the old-fashioned church of St. Mary, the only English place of worship in the little Welsh town; and there flocked in the Davieses—Mrs. Davies, with her white, cold face, and pink satin bonnet; and the great Jones family, who had come in their carriage; and then the tradespeople, who vied with each other, and with the high and mighty in the gaiety and splendour of their clothes; and there were the Perfectways, desperately perfect.

Paul watched the line of white bonnets and proper faces which appeared at the top of their pew. He thought of Emma, whom soon the untempted, unimpeachable, little milliners would dare to despise and scorn. He looked then into the aisle and noted the old grey headed men, and aged women in men's hats, and the troop of Sunday school children, which last were not at all perfect in their conduct, for they whispered, and tittered, and stared, and passed marbles and faded flower-stalks into one another's hands, after the fashion of Sunday school children all the world over; and then the organ struck up, and the Rev. Mr. Holding mounted into the reading-desk, and service commenced,—"If we say that we have no sin, we deceive ourselves, and the truth is not in us; but if we confess our sins, God is faithful and just to forgive us our sins, and to cleanse us from all unrighteousness." You see, these words are encouraging to those who, like Paul, feel that they have a great deal of unconfessed, unforgiven sin to answer for; and I believe that he joined as heartily as anybody in St. Mary's in the confession which forms so beautiful a part of our church service—more heartily, perhaps, than the Perfectways; but then, to be sure, the words of the exhortation could not be supposed to apply to them, but only to trespassers, like Paul and Emma. When the service was over, Mr. Holding, who was a meek-faced curate and a good man, mounted into the pulpit and gave out the text, " Not until seven times, but until seventy times seven."

Paul almost started when the sweet words which bore so wonderfully on his own case were spoken by the preacher. The divine nature of forgiveness—its God-like attributes, our own sure need of mercy, were dwelt on by the curate in a manner strong, simple, affectionate.

I suppose some of the Aberglace folks may have gone home feeling a little less rancorous for the nonce against some others of their neighbours. Perhaps Mrs. Davies may have magnanimously resolved to pardon

Mrs. Jones for not inviting her to her son's grand ball, when he attained his majority; and Mr. Shortman, the draper, may have hesitated to whether he would send that very cutting article to the Aberglace "Looker On," which was so completely to nonplus Mr. Sugarton, the grocer. And Paul? His eyes were wet before he left the church, and he felt almost as though his own great need of mercy should induce him thoroughly to forgive, even to pray for his cruel foe. I do not say that Paul proceeded to this length, but I do say that he came out of church with gentler, better feelings, and with no wild thirst for further vengeance. He dined alone on his return to Doctor Milton's, and after that he went out among his poorer patients for an hour or two, and then turned towards home again, purposing to write to Emma, whom he supposed by this time to be under the care of her mother. Just as he stepped into the passage at Doctor Milton's, a note in a strange writing was put into his

hand, he broke the seal and read as
follows :—

Come at once, your sister is prematurely delivered of a
boy, she is in danger, come at once. I send my own little
pony and phæton by the lad who brings you this.
M. WILLIAMS,
Bithol.

Crushing the note in his hand Paul asked
the servant where the boy was to be found
who had brought the note. She told him
at the Bull, and thither he hastened, where
·he found the pony carriage, and a boy who
could not speak English. He hired a
horse from the inn, and he rode out of
Aberglace. He rode the eighteen miles
in silence and in dread; and when he
again approached Bithol, the autumn twilight had fallen. Madame Williams met
him at the door, he could not see her
face, but she took his hand in hers, and
said in a faint whisper "too late."

"Great God of Heaven!" said Paul in
a tone deep and fearful, "You don't mean,
you can't mean?"

"She is gone," said Madame Williams,

leading him into her parlour, where there
was a lamp burning.

Paul's face worked, it was blanched to a
frightful pallor, and his grey eyes sparkled
with an expression that was not love, nor
grief, nor pity, nor rage, nor thirst for
vengeance, but was a mixture of all. "Not
dead," he broke forth at last, "Don't say
that, its not true, you know it can't be true
so soon, you mistake, let me look, let me
go, I tell you she's not dead."

Madame Williams calmly took the lamp
in her hand, and laid the other on that
of Paul. There was but little softening in
her worldly face, but little as there was,
it humanized the expression of her eyes.
"Don't take it so to heart," she said, "she
died quietly, and without pain, better
than a life of shame. I did what I could.
I did indeed, and so did Sarah."

"She can't be dead you know," Paul
went on in a hollow whisper, "it's not possible."

Madame Williams took him upstairs, into

a neat chamber, with dark polished floor, and a small bed, with white hangings, and there Emma lay dead!!!

The "sad, shrouded eye," half closed; the marble-like, still hand; the lip, with its haughty curve all gone, parted slightly, fixed. And she had passed away early that afternoon it seemed, before the message could have reached Paul, and she was dead, gone, beyond the power of earthly forgiveness, or pity, or sorrow, or mourning, or blame.

It was a common tale. She had died from exhaustion. She had died suddenly, without pain, without consciousness, without fear. The young, warm, breathing life, that had been so flooded with the waters of affliction, so blighted by the storms of earthly passions, so darkened by the clouds of poverty, and sorrow, and want; the young warm breathing life was merged into eternity, the passionate, proud heart was stilled for ever, the sweet, scornful young voice was hushed into an awful silence, and Emma lay dead!!!

Paul did not speak a word. He took up the chill hand, and held it in his own, then let it drop, and turned away his face. A great change passed over his whole being. His fair, dead sister, who would soon be hidden from his sight, did not awaken one throe of revengeful longing. Overwhelmed with a sorrow which would, he knew, henceforth shadow his whole life, his first feelings were of love to those who remained to him on earth, not of revenge towards the sin stained betrayer of Emma.

"If *he* could see her now, he would grieve, he would pity, he would repent,' exclaimed Paul. "He is human, after all, and his remorse will be frightful. God forgive him for his enormous crime. God preserve me from the like. Oh, my mother! my dear mother! This will kill you," and the strong man sobbed in his agony.

"It is best as it is," said Madame Williams, at length, in a calm, almost a kind tone. "She is at rest now."

"Yes," returned Paul, bitterly. "That

rest which remains for us all at the last, that stillness which is not repose, that peace which is made of unconsciousness and nothingness. Oh, Emma! my little fair-haired sister."

He turned away, and left the room, and Madame Williams followed him down stairs. By the fire, in the parlour, old Sarah was nursing a tiny specimen of humanity, a wailing feeble infant, and the old crone was rocking to and fro, and crooning aloud a melancholy ditty, which went nigh to driving Paul mad. "Bye, by, baby, by," sung old Sarah, and then the weak mite in her arms cried faintly. Paul did not look at the child. He was thinking of his mother, and of how to break the awful news to her without causing her death. He knew her excitability, and trembled for the result.

"I cannot tell her," he broke out, at length. "This must remain for ever unspoken, if the words are to come from me. Is there no pitying soul, no one with some feeling of feminine gentleness to be met with?" And then he thought of Margaret Percy. Suppose she were told this sad history. Would she sympathise, would she pity a mother who was so humble as Mrs. Withers? Oh, no! She would think Paul presumptuous, impertinent, to dare to talk to her in that way, to dare to ask *her* for sympathy. Miss Percy, of Percy Priory, would most likely deem her small ivory ears polluted by the mention of a being so lost, so frail, as she who lay dead up-stairs. In imagination, Paul heard her few cold words of condolence, saw her little startled look of horror, and her pretty proud mouth, with its intense expression of hauteur, its lips, which seemed formed to tell Paul Withers of the great gulf which was fixed between Margaret Percy and himself.

No, she must not be spoken to; and then he thought of a certain sweet young countenance, upon which his eyes had rested not a week back. Who was that girl? No matter who or what she was. He would seek her, and she should go and comfort his mother. She would go, he knew it, without reasoning, without any grounds for his conviction, beyond the remembrance of the heavenly face shaded by brown hair. He woke from his reverie with a start.

"Madame Williams, who is that young lady, with a face like an angel, who sometimes visits at Percy Priory? She rides a black horse, and her hair falls on her shoulders. Do you know her?"

"Oh, that is Miss Heartley, the rector's daughter. The rectory is not far from here."

"Then I will go there. I want to speak to Miss Heartley."

"Are you mad?"

"No, I think not, unless sorrow has crazed me. But I wish to ask Miss Heartley to go and comfort my mother."

"Stop one moment. There is a Mrs. Heartley?"

"Yes."

"The mother you know?"

"Yes."

"You must see her first. She is an English-woman, highly bred and highly educated."

"Well?"

"She is a sad invalid, confined mostly to her couch through a weakness in the spine. Between this mother and daughter subsists that perfect unity which you would sneer at in a novel as absurd; but it is in this case genuine."

"The more will they sympathise with the suffering mother of a dead child."

"But Mrs. Heartley's morality is of the strictest, her tone of mind of the highest, her notions of purity the most *recherché*. Quite a Miss Edgworth in morals."

"Is she? Then the greater will be her sympathy for a poor soiled child like Emma."

"Do you think so? These pure reli-gious people are sometimes very hard and cruel."

"The mother of that face I saw last week is not hard or cruel, I know. I will go there."

" Not to-night."

" Yes, to-night."

" Mrs. Heartley will be in bed."

Paul sat down, and tears forced their way through his fingers, which he entwined over his eyes.

" Here, swallow a glass of wine."

Paul shook his head. "The only thing I am capable of, Mrs. Williams, is to walk up and down all night. I cannot rest."

" Absurd. You walked all last night. No human being can stand such exertion. Come, I insist upon your lying on that sofa. Sleep will come ; but take the wine first— come—come. Fretting won't make it any better."

" If you was to cry your blessed eyes hout of yer ed yer couldent bring the little ooman back," remarked Sarah, sagely, and then she went on crooning, " Bye, bye, baby. Bye, bye, bye."

" Will you go away ?" said Paul, suddenly turning upon the woman. " If I am to drink that wine, and lie on that couch,

I hope you will go away. Now, I do, indeed."

"Go away, Sarah," said Madame Williams. "Take the child to your own room, and keep it warm."

Old Sarah turned back. "The two women is coming at ten to-morrow fur to lay out the corpse. Minds as your up in time," and she went off.

She was one of those agreeable people to whom the laying out of a corpse is an exciting and refreshing amusement. When she was gone, Madame Williams made Paul drink the wine, and then she compelled him to lie on the sofa.

"You will sleep," she said, and she was right. Paul slept, and he dreamed a strange dream. It was of Charles Roggmoore. He saw a hole, like a grave, in which he knew that Emma lay, and that there she would remain until the last trump should sound, but he thought that Charles Roggmoore was buried with her alive, and that he was calling on him loudly for mercy.

"Let me out, Paul," he said, "and I will be a different man. Let me out, and I will repent," and Paul strove to answer him, strove to help him, but found his power of speech and movement gone. He awoke with a start. It was broad day. His sleep must have been dreamless the first part of the night. It was now the sixth day of the eventful week that he had given to Emma. He could not bear to wait for the coming of the women who were to smooth and straighten the limbs of his dead sister. He went into the yard, where he washed his pale and haggard face at the pump, and so went at once to Heartley Rectory.

He was not very long in finding his way to the pretty cottage. It was a fine September morning, and Mrs. Heartley's being a complaint which required a vast amount of sitting in the open air, it so happened that when Paul pushed back the iron gate, and began to walk up the gravel, he saw Mrs. Heartley and Flora sitting beneath the shade of a branching beech upon the lawn. There was a table, spread with breakfast things, before them.

"Who is that, Flora love?" asked the mother.

"Its the young doctor that attends at the Percies, mamma. The young man whom I told you I took quite a fancy to in the park the other day. Now look at him. Hasn't he a noble, good face? Why, he's coming here," and Paul came right up to the ladies, and bowed low.

"I cannot apologise for this intrusion," he stammered out, "for it admits of no apology. But I think I appeal to kind hearers."

Flora handed him a chair, and Mrs. Heartley, in the kindest, sweetest tone, begged him not to be under the least fear, and then he told his tale, warming with indignation at some parts, and now and then fairly breaking down in his recital, and the mother and daughter wept with him and comforted him.

Mrs. Heartley's indignation at the conduct of Mr. Roggmoore was excessive. She
was a woman of little more than forty, fair
and beautiful still, but more woman than
angel after all, by which I would convey
that she was a true woman, tender, loving,
trustful, something in disposition like Paul's
grandmother, only that her birth was gentle,
and her refinement excessive.

Flora felt pity for all, even for the bad
man who had done such deadly wrong.
Her mother wanted that bad man shamed
and punished. Miss Percy, she declared,
was no fit companion for her child if, after
all this, she persisted in accepting Mr.
Roggmoore.

Flora glanced furtively at Paul's pale
face, and liked its expression better than
ever. He looked at her, and across the fire
of his love for Margaret Percy there passed
a chilling doubt—he knew not what—but
the lovely face before him seemed to claim
the highest place in his admiration. Cold,
hard, statue-like, Margaret could never have

looked half so divine as that fair creature before him.

I intend to pass over the scene that followed this. The carriage was ordered, and the Heartleys, mother and daughter, went to Roggmoore Lodge, and took Paul with them. He did not go into the room with them, nor into the house, but lingered in the grounds. He heard the mother's shriek of agony, he heard the soothing, pitying voices of the good Samaritans, and then he rushed in, and flung his arms round his mother.

"Mother, mother, I will be all to you, work for you, cherish you, comfort you. You shall come to London. Don't cry so, mother. Emma is happier than she would have been alive. There is a dear child too."

*　　*　　*　　*　　*

That evening Paul returned to Aberglace again on foot. He went to give orders for his sister's simple funeral; to pay his trifling debts, to order mourning to be sent to Roggmoore Lodge. Aberglace had got hold of the tale, and was handling it in ungenerous fashion. The Withers' had laid a plot, and it served them right that it had failed. That sulky, unsociable young fellow, indeed, to dare to knock Mr. Roggmoore down; and the girl, she was running in and out of Mr. Percy's house all the day before she died, insulting them, although Mr. Percy was so ill. And her mother was a plotter, and she a poor fool, and Paul a regular brute. So Aberglace wagged its head, and rattled its tongue, and the Perfectways observed, that if a great gentleman had made *love* to *them* they should have known that he could not mean honourably. And Mrs. Davies said it was what she had expected. And Paul went seriously about ordering the mourning, and paying his bills, and then he went to bed, and the next morning the week was up. He rose and strolled on the beach in the early bright sunshine, and looked, as he was never tired of looking, at the now placid waters of the glorious bay, and then he turned towards home again. He rung the bell. The door was opened by a tall, brawny policeman, another started forward, and the two clenched his shoulders.

" What is the matter ?" asked Paul.

" We arrest you," said the first, " on the charge of murder, the murder of Charles Bingham Roggmoore, Esq., of Roggmoore Lodge."

CHAPTER V.

WHAT THE PAPERS SAID.

"FRIGHTFUL MURDER IN WALES.—Last week the inhabitants of Aberglace, a pretty town on the coast, in Craigshire, Wales, were thrown into a dreadful state of excitement by the news that a gentleman of high standing in the neighbourhood had been savagely murdered. The circumstances of the case are of an exaggerated barbarity, and accompanied by facts which go far towards increasing the already very great prejudice which exists against the supposed murderer. Charles Bingham

Roggmoore, Esq., of Roggmoore Park, in the county of Hants, and Altgloss Castle, in Invernesshire, a gentleman of cultivated mind, fine person, and polished manners, has been ruthlessly slaughtered, it is suspected by an assistant surgeon to a Doctor Milton, a physician of some eminence, formerly in London, and at present very justly esteemed in Wales, where he has retired for his health. Paul Withers, the suspected murderer, is a tall, stalwart young man of three or four and twenty; his origin is supposed to be rather obscure, and it seems that he received his education at the hands of a charitable stranger, who picked him up when a child on London Bridge, where he was officiating as a shoe black, but the old adage of the silk purse and the sow's ear appears to have been amply verified in this case. Little is known at present of his student life, but it is believed that he is of fair average ability as regards his profession. It is, however, with his subsequent conduct, since he commenced the world for himself, that we have to do now. During the time of his residence with the excellent medical gentleman alluded to above, he has rendered himself abhorrent to the inhabitants of Aberglace and its neighbourhood, by his sulky unbending behaviour, and rude rough manners. Nothing, however, partaking of the deadly nature of the crime now imputed to him, was suspected of Paul Withers up to Monday week, when the bloody deed was discovered to have been perpetrated, of which he appears to be guilty.

"The mother of Withers resided as housekeeper at the shooting box of the murdered gentleman, who came down with his brother occasionally in the autumn for shooting of wild ducks, &c. There was a daughter in the case, a creature frail and fair. The seductive arts of this syren were put into execution, doubtless, with the concurrence of mother and son. Aberglace being only five miles from Roggmoore Lodge, the plotting mother and son had many opportunities of laying their heads together, and the design appears to have been, to bring about a marriage between the housekeeper's daughter and the young and nobly born master of the house: the plot failed, Mr. Roggmoore awakened to a sense of what was due to himself and his family, and resolved to break off a connexion already fraught with shame and sin. He wished to provide for the unprincipled young woman, and to leave her altogether. Into the house of a gentleman of very high standing, none other than Cecil Percy, of Percy Priory, M.P. for Craigshire, who was at that time seriously ill, the shameless girl, Withers' sister, had the effrontery to pursue her victim. Withers, who was in the house in his medical capacity, happened to come into the room when Mr. Roggmoore was protesting against this intrusion, and, gathering from the tenor of the words spoken by the unfortunate gentleman, that the ambitious schemes of himself and his family were seen through and frustrated, the in-

temperate and savage young man sprung
upon Mr. Roggmoore in a perfect frenzy of
brutal rage, knocked out his front tooth,
and laid him insensible upon the floor.
He used also some very terrible threats,
swearing he would have the life blood of
Mr. Roggmoore, and in frightful terms
assuring him that hell should not shield him
from his revenge.   The butler thrust him
from the house, and his sister followed him,
and respecting the dark deeds of that night,
nothing is positively known save the horrible
and ghastly result.   Mr. Roggmoore left
Percy Priory at one o'clock on the evening of Saturday mounted on his own horse,
and he has never been seen alive since.
Withers went with his sister to the house of
a lady in the neighbourhood, a Madame
Williams.   This lady offered him a bed for
the night, which courtesy he roughly refused, alleging that he preferred to walk
the eighteen miles into Aberglace, although
it was then nearly 9 o'clock at night. He
set off on his lonely walk; and it is true

that he had no weapon in his hands, but certainly with a *case of instruments* in his pocket. On Sunday morning he presented himself before his employer, to whom, in a voice of rage, he related his savage assault on his unhappy victim. The doctor remonstrated with him on the violence of his passions; and then the man *actually went to church*, which looks very like trying to cover his crimes by a cloak of hypocrisy. Meanwhile Mr. Roggmoore was not missed, because, at Roggmoore Lodge, he was supposed to have been at Percy Priory, and at Percy Priory he was believed to have been at Roggmoore Lodge; but in the afternoon of Monday, his valet, going up to Mr. Percy's and hearing that his master had started for his own house on the Saturday night, an alarm was raised. The horse of the unhappy gentleman was discovered browsing on the hills, and early on Tuesday morning an appalling and alarming proof of the murder came to light. In a retired part of the mountain, within a few yards of

where Withers must have passed in his
lonely night walk, a huge sack has been
found, in which are the mutilated, defaced
remains of a human body, evidently dissevered by *surgical instruments*.   There
were no clothes in the sack, save a pair of
blood-stained riding gloves, identified as
having belonged to Mr. Roggmoore.   The
very face of the victim was so cut as to leave
no traces of humanity, so to speak, about it.
None but a practised hand could have so
hacked and hewed the human form divine;
but Withers has doubtless often indulged
before in this pastime, when a student at
Guy's.   He was taken into custody at
Aberglace on Tuesday, a few hours after
the discovery of the body, and is now
lodged at the gaol of Cragton.   He mani-
fests the most dogged and sullen indifference, and refuses to see the chaplain, or to
answer any questions.   The murdered gentleman was heir to an earldom, and his loss
will be deeply felt by a large circle of ad-
miring friends."

This was what a provincial paper said.
Now I'll tell you what the *Times* said :—

"THE CRAIGSHIRE MURDER.—Crimes,
which to think of make men shudder in their
beds, are, happily, of late, of comparatively
rare occurrence; but this dark deed on the
Welsh mountains reminds one of some German
legend. We have all the accompaniments.
A night of alternate moonlight and
cloud, a lonely stretch of pine clad mountain,
a fierce, unscrupulous nature, panting
eagerly with the desire of that " wild
justice," called revenge, watching, if all
surmises be true, for the coming of the
expected foe; for foe the gentleman of
"thirty descents" had certainly been to the
roughly reared young surgeon, who, it is
to be feared, has taken human life in the
frenzy of his mad rage and disappointed
feelings. If it be true that from the crimes
and follies of our neighbours we ought to
derive lessons for the guidance of our own
conduct, and the avoidance of such crimes
in ourselves, there can be no harm in dwell-

ing a little on this frightful story, and attempting to analyze the motives and the passions which may have swayed the supposed murderer. At a time like the present, when the difficulty of marrying their daughters is an acknowledged grievance among some of the higher classes, at a time when "love," in its purest essence, appears almost ignored, and the desire of forming a wealthy alliance is, or seems to be, the chief object of every young and beautiful woman, when most mothers, like the one in Locksley Hall, set themselves to the task of "preaching down their daughters' hearts by dint of a little host of maxims," amid which the oft repeated words, suitable, desirable, satisfactory, bear reference to "filthy lucre," more than to home, affection, sympathy, or love; what shall we say of a plotting housekeeper, who sets her pretty daughter as a snare to entrap a young gentleman, whom half the mothers in May Fair would have welcomed with rapture as a suitor to their fair patrician daughters?

The brother enters warmly into the scheme, the brother, whose childhood and early life have been passed amid the dregs of low London life, the brother, who has slept under dry arches, and herded with thieves and pickpockets, who has starved upon a crust, and who would perhaps long ago have finished his sad career of ignorance and vice in the manner one would naturally suppose probable, had the charity of a gentleman not lifted him from this obscurity, and given him an education, even a profession. The wild instincts were, however, untamed, the savage nature unsubdued, the scheming, cunning desire of obtaining more than was just or right remained in Paul Withers. He finds his sister disgraced instead of raised. Let us give him, too, some credit for humane feeling and affection. The butler stated that the girl, when driven from the door, ran into her brother's arms, and that he sheltered her in them kindly. The poor girl is since dead, but her death did not occur until after the murder of Mr. Roggmoore, so that her brother was not avenging her death, if he did murder him, but only her dishonour. The details of the story are almost too sickening to be dwelt upon. They remind one of the German book, of which it has been said, '*Er lasst sich nicht lesen,*'—that it would not suffer itself to be read. How the two men met, whether the life of Mr. Roggmoore was taken by treachery, or whether he engaged in that deadly fight to which Withers challenged him, is not known, for the prisoner maintains his innocence, and utter ignorance of the whole affair; but the human body, entire in itself, chopped up by an experienced hand, is now undergoing medical examination; it was only beginning to decompose when discovered on the Tuesday. It is evidently that of a man, and a tall man, as was Mr. Roggmoore. The face is horribly disfigured, the eyes being scooped out and the nose hacked off completely; the hair had been actually singed off the scalp, which might easily have been done by means of a lighted match. Nature sickens over these abhorrent details; humanity shudders, and ladies faint; but from all this there is a lesson to be learned. Scheming mothers, take care first of your children's hearts before you think of selling them for rank. Young men of fashion, too, who will shrink from the details of young Roggmoore's story, will do well to pause in their pursuit of dissipation, and to '*remember the end.*' We cannot award the unqualified praise which some of our contemporaries have given to the memory of this young gentleman, whose greatest recommendations appear to have been his enormous wealth and his expected earldom."

This was what the *Times* said. Other papers, of less note, either chimed in with its remarks or set themselves against it by quibbling over some of its arguments, or attempting to sneer down its sentiments. Not one took up the cudgels for Paul, not one voice was raised for his defence.

"The prisoner Withers is to be tried at the Central Criminal Court, to avoid any prejudice that might exist against him from his Craigshire contemporaries. The greatest excitement prevails everywhere."— *Midland Gazette.*

"It is currently reported that the prisoner Withers is the nephew of a rich attorney in St. Clements county, but the report is not as yet authenticated."—*St. Clements Guardian.*

"We are, unhappily for the credit of our town, obliged to admit that Withers is a native of this place, being the second son of the late Leetham Withers, and grandson of the late J. Withers, of the Orchards, in this county."—*St. Clements Looker In.*

And this is just a little, reader, of what the papers said.

CHAPTER VI.

WHAT THE PERCIES SAID.

CONVALESCENT, Mr. Percy sat reading the papers by the fire one evening, towards the close of the old year; he sat on a luxurious chair, his feet resting on an ermine foot-stool, his wine and fruit spread near him on the table. Opposite to him on a low seat was his fair child Margaret, engaged in knitting; she was not a whit changed since we last saw her; still pale, passionless, composed; still with the serious, blue eyes, and the firm haughty mouth. Mr. Percy put down the newspaper and sighed.

"Don't you feel well, papa?"

"Oh yes, Margaret, but I am tired of this Withers case. I wish it was fairly over, and the fellow hung out of the way."

Miss Percy gave a little shudder. "I don't wish that."

"Why? Don't you believe him guilty?"

"The evidence is, unhappily, so conclusive that I dare not say that. I fear he is guilty."

"And you don't wish him hanged?"

"Well, no. I think not," said Margaret, fastening her thread.

"I don't like hanging, but if people deserve it?"

"If it comes to that, papa, a great many deserve hanging."

"And don't get it! which makes me rejoice all the more that one rascal should get his deserts. Poor Charles! such a fine fellow as he was."

"Yes, papa. It is a terrible thing to reflect upon. Still, I suppose poor Charles had behaved ill to the girl?"

"Not a bit of it. Could you expect a gentleman to marry a low girl?"

"Certainly not," said Margaret, calmly. "A mésalliance is, of all things, the action for which I have the least sympathy, the least tolerance. But Charles was not called upon to deceive the girl?"

"Well, poor fellow, he paid dearly for his folly, and now I hope his murderer will be brought to justice."

"Well, papa, I suppose the law must take its course. I am not going to take up the cudgels for the doctor's assistant in the way that Flora and her mother do; they really go too far, they make the young man into a hero and a martyr, and Flora actually cries if he is mentioned. She is a sweet, sensible child, but too much overburdened with feeling and sentiment, and beautiful indignation, and that sort of thing. She'll grow wiser some day, I suppose. Shall I ring for tea?"

And this was what the Percies said, reader; and between you and me I have come to the conclusion that Miss Percy was about right when she gave it out that she had no heart; and as to the serious, tender look in the eyes, I am inclined to think that if Paul or Flora either had looked deeper down into their blue depths, they would have discovered that the expression was mere surface after all; a pretty, earnest look, that meant nothing. Poor Paul had indeed sacrificed to a thankless idol.

CHAPTER VII.

WHAT FELIX SAID.

One day before the new year came in, there was a grand ball given at the house of a city merchant, whose purple pomp was blazoned forth gorgeously in his great west-end mansion. He had singers from the opera, a French *chef-de-cuisine*, to whom he paid two hundred pounds for the night's work, a score of gaudy footmen, a military band. His saloons were decked up as though for royalty; and amongst the bankers and merchant princes who attended the ball, there was a pretty fair sprinkling of sprigs of nobility; there were artists of all kinds to be met with; there were lovely women and stately men; there was card playing; and there were authors, and poets, and wit, and beauty, and wealth. All were assembled in the great golden house in the great square; all went merry as a marriage bell.

Outside, the snow lay thick and white; the keen wind uprose and whistled sharply round the street corners; the homeless children crouched under doorways; the policemen, wrapped up warmly, went shivering along their beats; the drunkards alone seemed to derive inspiration from the cold, they shouted out snatches of songs hilariously. And then the snow began to fall again, thickly, softly, silently; the capes of the policemen were heavy with the white covering, and the streets became deserted, and still the snow fell.

About twelve o'clock a cab drove up to the door of the gold and purple merchant, and a man sprung out, and, after paying the cabman and giving his card to the footman, he began to ascend the wide, gilded staircase, and he elbowed his way into the ballroom, hung with velvet and golden stars, where the band was executing a delightful waltz, and some graceful dancers were turning round in time to the measured cadence; and among the dancers was a striking couple, young and brilliantly handsome. The man was perhaps five and twenty; tall, graceful, artistic in his every movement; wanting, I suppose, in the "*je ne sais quoi*" of the patrician; not, in fact, "*un homme comme il faut,*" so to speak, but more richly gifted by nature than any possessor of blue blood in the room. He was dark, that is, of a rich, soft olive complexion; a clear glow on the well-formed cheek, glossy jet black hair, neither too short nor too long, but arranged with consummate skill; a perfect Greek profile, a coal black moustache; large, mournful, magnificent dark eyes. In short, dear young lady reader, he was what you would consider a perfect duck of a man.

All ladies admire dark men you know; and when the dark man, like Louis Quatorze, waltzes like an angel, and has tender dark eyes, a perfect profile, and a black moustache, he becomes perfectly irresistible—quite dangerous—so keep out of his way young lady; he is charming, but your mamma would never sanction his addresses. He is only a struggling artist, not very rich, nor as yet very famous, only very handsome, very extravagant, and very fond of—what? Any particular fair one? Well, no. That flaxen-haired, blue-eyed, pink-cheeked, pretty young creature he is waltzing with is the only child of the golden merchant, and, like Miss Dinah, famed in song, is "sixteen years old," and "with a very large fortune in silver and gold." But the perfect diamond duck with the black moustache has never seen her before, so I cannot take upon me to state that he is very fond of her as yet. What is he

fond of, then? Horse-racing? No. Painting? He was once, but he has not sufficient
love for his art to cling to it for its own
sake. He finds it slow work getting rich
at it. Well, does he like country sports,
town dissipation, literature, love, gaiety,
fashion, eating, drinking, or dancing?
Does he love nature, poetry, reality,
scandal, his mother, travelling, the Continent, Paris, the Alps, or jam pudding?
You see, we all of us have a predeliction
for something or somebody; and now,
which of these did the handsome artist
like? Whisper low. It's bad manners in
good society, I know; but still, just for
once, and as you take such an overwhelm
ing interest in the dark young man, polished
by foreign travel, who is twirling round so
gracefully!!! I'll tell you what he likes.
His name is Felix Withers, and he loves
"himself." There, it's out now; and of
course I don't mean to infer that Felix is at
all singular in his preference. Numbers of
others are similarly situated with regard

to their affections. And so the band plays on till the dancers are tired, and Felix leads Miss Goldenheart to a couch, and brings her an ice.

The man who came in so late to the ball is a far more famous artist than Felix. He sells his paintings for 800 guineas at a time. You have seen him twice or thrice before, I think, reader—once on Waterloo Bridge, six years ago exactly it will be to-nght, one day before the new year. You remember his strongly-built frame, his tawny whiskers, his auburn hair, fresh-coloured cheeks, and hazel eyes, don't you? He is dressed for a ball. You see him now in black, with a white cravat and white gloves. All he does is to watch Felix Withers and the flaxen-haired heiress; and Felix, as yet, does not perceive him. Presently a young guardsman saunters up to the young lady and claims her promised hand for a quadrille, and Felix saunters round by himself. Then our friend Reginald crosses over to him and accosts him—

"Then it's really true you are here, Withers?"

Felix looked so handsome when he blushed, and now he really was quite enchanting in his graceful embarrassment. "Oh, Mr. Wylde! how d'ye do?"

"Excessively well, thank you, Mr. Withers," said Reginald, giving him his hand, and looking him steadily in the face. "I was not invited to this ball."

"Were you not? Oh, never mind! Mr. Goldenheart will be delighted to see you. I am sure he didn't know you had returned from Greece."

"I only returned this morning."

"Oh!" said Felix, pulling a flower-stalk to pieces.

"And the terrible news about Paul only reached me last week. I am such a bad correspondent that no one knew where to direct to me. A chance newspaper revealed the whole to me, and I hastened back."

"Oh!" said Felix again, squeezing the flower-stalk very hard.

"I enquired first for him; I saw him."
Reginald's lip trembled, and he bit it hard,
and then went on again. "He told me his
mother had been kindly cared for by some
good people in Craigshire. She has taken
lodgings near Paul, and visits him daily. I
wonder her excitability does not kill Paul
and herself also."

"Indeed!" said Felix in a low tone,
"it's most terrible to me. I've not seen
him, of course, and I contrive to keep out
of my mother's way. I should never be
noticed at all if it were suspected that I was
connected with the Withers, the murderer.
Fortunately, we have seen so little of each
other of late years, that I think it's not
known at all. I should not be asked here
if it were!!! It's a horrible affair. Pray
don't speak of it in a tone above a whisper.
Walls have ears, you know."

"A fact in architectural history that I
was not aware of," said Reginald, drily;
"and I suppose it is a phantasy to imagine
that all men have some human feeling.

At any rate, you appear to be an exception."

"Mr. Wylde," said Felix, touching his arm, "you're rich; you've made your fortune. It can be no disgrace for you to admit that you were Paul's first patron; but poor me, just struggling up, it's very hard—it is, indeed!!! I deny everywhere that I am any connexion of the Withers's, and if you disgrace me I'll go abroad. What rich girl would marry a murderer's brother?"

Reginald gave a long, low, whistle, which was very ill-behaved in a ball-room, and then he glanced in the direction of Miss Goldenheart. "I honor your prudence, your self-possession. I envy the temperament that places you beyond the reach of any human sufferings not absolutely physical. I am here to study you as a model of unconcern. You should have lived in the reign of terror, Sir. Your stoical qualifications would have had ample opportunity for display. You might have danced at a ball while the tumbril was carrying your mother to execution in the next street. Good night, Mr. Felix. Go on and prosper."

Now you know what Felix Withers said.

CHAPTER VIII.

THE TRIAL OF PAUL WITHERS.

THE winter has rolled away with its dark days and bitter nights, and dense, damp fogs. The poor have starved, the rich have feasted; school-boys have suffered considerably from chilblains; children in courts and alleys have suffered considerably from cold and hunger. At last, however, it is gone, or nearly so; and it is an early, bright, and mild Spring, and everybody is very cheerful, and very much pleased, because there is a great murder case to be tried; and everybody is confident that the young man will be hung, which is a comforting reflection to those who don't feel in any danger of a like catastrophe—it makes their safety complete bliss in comparison.

"Thursday week the trial is to come on?"

"Yes."

"And who is for the prosecution?"

"Blackett."

"Ah, and he will black it too, and no mistake." And Figly, the grocer in the Borough, winks hard and bursts into a loud laugh. He thinks he has made a pun, you see; and he intends to accompany his friend Pennypot, the chemist, to the Central Criminal Court on Thursday week, and to leave his shop to the young gentleman with smooth, sandy hair, who stands behind his counter.

"And who is for the prisoner?"

"Goodness knows! Mr. Wylde, the gentleman who is interesting himself so much for him, has tried to secure Ferret; but he won't come under a great sum—

more than the gentleman feels able to pay."

"He will want some one with a good head against Blackett," remarked Mr. Pennypot, gravely.

Figly snapped his fingers. "Twenty Ferrets couldn't save him, Sir. He is dead already." And Figly stuck a pen behind his ear, and looked important.

"Well, good morning," said Pennypot, blandly. "I shall be here early on Thursday week."

"Yes, yes, Sir" (people of Figly's stamp always interlard their discourse plentifully with the word, Sir). "Yes, yes, Sir; come early and take a bit of breakfast with us. We must be in time to get good places. Compliments to your good lady. Won't she come too?"

"No. She can't leave our young folks," said Pennypot, gently; "but I shall have to tell her all about it."

"Good morning, Sir."

And the grocer and the chemist shook

hands warmly over the expected pleasure which was to terminate so agreeably in the hanging of Paul.

If you have never been to Appleton, in the midland counties, reader, you have missed seeing one of the prettiest little towns in England. But if you want to see it in its glory you should visit it two months later, in the month of May; for then its old-fashioned gable-ended houses seem buried in a world of white blossoms; and the rich forest trees, which grow everywhere in the fields, are robed in their first green vesture,

One bright evening in March a gentleman drove up to the Apple-tree Inn, in Appleton. He had taken a fly from the nearest railway station, and he brought a carpet bag with him. He was going to sleep at the Apple-tree that night. We know the gentleman well. We know his tawny whisker and his hazel eye. His ruddy cheek is somewhat paler since we last saw him. It only wants three days to

Paul's trial. Reginald did not, as was his wont when he visited out of the way places, begin to question the landlord about the picturesque points of view in the neighbourhood. He asked nothing about the church, with its mullion windows; nothing about the farm houses that had been monasteries, and which stand deep amid the woods and orchards in St. Clements county, with their time-honoured gables and lattice-paned windows shining in the sunbeams. Reginald asked no questions that an artist would or should have asked. No; he called for a glass of ale and a chop, and when he had finished his meal he asked the landlord one simple question—"Where does Mr. Jacob Withers, the lawyer, live?"

"Up at the top of the Hill-road, Sir. A large red house, with a green verandah round it, Sir."

"All right; but where is the Hill-road?"

"Straight up, Sir. If you leave this

house and turn to your left you can't miss it."

"All right," said Reginald again, and he set out for the evening walk up the hill-top road.

It was moonlight now, and the air was balmy as spring itself. It had been one of those days we are indulged with sometimes in March, when early spring seems to have borrowed a day from the coming summer; and Reginald walked up the hill road which winds among goodly fields and orchards; and if it had not been for a great care at his heart he would have enjoyed the stroll. At last he came to the red house with the green verandah. It had a lovely lawn in front, and gardens and conservatories behind. It looked a sleek, smooth, fat, well to do, substantial house, from the plate-glass windows in the dining room to the large, bright, brass knocker on the door; and Reginald grasped the knocker, and gave a loud rat-tat on the well painted door.

A page opened it—a fat, respectable page, in blue cloth and buttons—and Reginald asked if Mr. Withers was in; and the fat, respectable page replied deferentially in the affirmative, and ushered Reginald into the breakfast room. He lighted a handsome lamp, and put it on the substantial mahogany table, and then, in an awful whisper, he asked for Reginald's name.

"Wylde. Mr. Wylde."

"Wylde, Sir."

"Yes," said Reginald, and the page went out. Presently he returned again.

"Please, sir, I've forgot what name it was as you said."

"Wylde, Wylde, Wylde," said Reginald, impatiently. "Think of wild ducks, or wild beasts. Shall I write it down?"

"Oh, Lord, no, sir," whimpered the page, with a frightened face. "Master ud be angery if he seed me a forgetting."

"You are afraid of your master," said Reginald, who began to see where the land lay.

The page warmed into familiarity. He winked hard, shrugged his shoulders, and observed, sententiously, "He's a regler boster of a chap. When he's angry, he'll make you shake in your shoes. Oh, my!" and the page went to the door, but returned once again.

"Wylde, sir."

"Yes, yes; pray be off; I'm in a hurry."

So the page went off, and Reginald had not long to wait before he heard the heavy tread of a man in the oil-clothed hall. The white china handle of the door turned round, and then Reginald stood in the presence of the Appleton lawyer—the man who had "got on."

Men of the provinces, who have lived all their lives away from the turmoil, the hurry, the refinement, the excitement, the enlightenment, let me add, of the great city, seem comparatively simple, even rude, when measured by the estimate of a man of the world like Reginald Wylde.

By rudeness, I would convey that primi-

tive ignorance of the higher arts of life
which is akin to simplicity, not to vulgarity.
The Appleton Lawyer, a great man at Appleton, respected in the county, and looked
up to by his clients, had never been more
than three times to London, and then only
for a week at a time. He had never read
much besides law and newspapers : he had
not time in his youth and now he had not
inclination. He was well dressed; scru-
pulously clean; his bow was sufficiently
studied. He seemed just a little nervous
before Reginald—he had no look of a gentleman about him (in Reginald's eyes, that
is to say—and it is now with his eyes that
we contemplate Jacob Withers): he had no
look of a gentleman about him, but he was
not the least vulgar. His face was pale,
and terribly aged and lined; the features
were large and roughly cast. There was a
dogged expression of determination about
the mouth, but the eyes were a lively pleasant hazel. His hair, what remained of it,
was a bright chesnut, but the top of the

head was bald.   He had no vulgarity in
the shape of rings and chains about him,
and he impressed the idea of a hard,
heavy, honest, matter-of-fact man, with few
sympathies and scanty refinement.

"I must introduce myself, Mr. Withers.
I have known you by name some time."

"Oh! indeed, Sir; please to sit down."

If you were to live a few months in St.
Clements county, I fancy that you would
have no difficulty ever afterwards in recog-
nising the accent of its natives.   It has a
most peculiar burr, unpleasant to those
whose earliest reminiscences are not asso-
ciated with that land of woodland and or-
chard as mine are.   I, for one, do not
wince at the sound of the voices of the St.
Clements county farmers even; but Reginald did not at all appreciate the accent of
Mr. Jacob Withers.   Mr. Jacob, who had
never lived for more than a fortnight out of
the county, and who spoke his native language quite grammatically, it is true, but in
a tone the reverse of polished.

"This uncle of Paul's is a common kind of man," was his first thought; which was not a just thought, for Jacob Withers is one of the most uncommon men of my acquaintance.

"Mr. Withers, I am totally unknown to you by reputation and name most probably. My name is Wylde, and I am an artist."

Mr. Withers looked rather as though that avowal had sunk his visitor a little in his estimation. His idea of an artist or an author was of a slightly contemptuous kind. He began to think that this person wanted money from him, and the sequel will show that he was not out in his reckoning.

"Oh, indeed, Sir," said Jacob Withers.

"I am most deeply interested in the impending trial of Paul Withers, your nephew."

Jacob Withers sprung to his feet, and struck the solid mahogany table loud with his open palm.

"Confound it all; is that your business?"

"Yes, I wish to lay the case before you."

"I'll hear nothing, nothing, nothing," said the Appleton lawyer, beginning to pace the Brussels carpet from the side window to the sideboard, and from the front window across to the fire-place, in which last hurried march he had to pass close by Reginald. "I'll not hear a word or speak a word on the subject, not one."

"Why not," asked Reginald bluntly. "You as a lawyer ought to know that there are two sides to every question. Let me give you my idea of the case. I have come a long way to speak to you. You will not be so uncourteous as to send me back without a hearing, surely, if you are a gentle-man."

The last shot told. The man who owned farms, some snug thousands in the bank, and the substantial red house he lived in, did not like to be considered other than a gentleman. He sat down.

"Well, Sir?"

"I like, respect, value your nephew.

He is an honest, honourable young man."

The Appleton lawyer's lip curled.

"An honourable young man," repeated Reginald firmly; "not a hero, perhaps, but ten times better at heart and in action than half the young men one meets with."

"That is your opinion."

"That is my conviction. A chain of circumstances appeared to have conspired against him, and in three days he is to be tried for his life charged with the murder of a man who had certainly wronged him terribly; but Paul is innocent of the murder."

The Appleton lawyer gave a grunt of dissent, and Reginald continued, "I am an artist, wild and extravagant. I have spent hundreds alas on idleness and folly within the last year, and at present I am rather poor in pocket. I don't feel able quite on my own account to discharge the heavy expenses of Paul's trial. I have done what I could; I have engaged Ferret for defence, and Quibble for his solicitor. Now I want you to advance, say two hundred pounds, towards the expenses; pay it to your own banker in Ferret's name."

Reginald spoke very coolly. The Appleton lawyer stared in wild amaze; he was too much astonished at his visitor's audacity to frame a reply at all. At last he burst forth, "You must take me, sir, for a consummate ass, a real fool."

"No, I take you to be the brother of Paul's father," said Reginald drily.

"Look here," said he of Appleton, wheeling about on his chair and facing Reginald, "long years ago, I swore I'd have nothing to do with that woman or her children."

"Your brother's children," observed Reginald.

"That woman," continued he of Appleton, disregarding Reginald's remark, "that woman has been a disgrace to me ever since I begun to get on; she got in debt, she wrote begging letters to my friends, she failed at St. Clements, she pestered me, she bothered me. I never answered her letters. I took no notice of her; then for the last six years I have had peace. Now the papers teem with the account of Withers, the murderer, and the whole county knows him to be my nephew. I believe him guilty, and I'll not give a penny, mark ye, towards his trial." And Jacob Withers stood up and glanced impatiently towards the door.

Reginald felt his wrath rising. The pale, blunt, hard determined lawyer had roused a regular tempest in the bosom of the noble, gentle, generous, large-souled artist. He turned upon him—

"Man, you are not worth a reply, not worthy of a taunt even. If you believe your Bible, which perhaps you do or perhaps you don't, you may in either case have heard of the promise which is held out to to the merciful—that they shall obtain mercy. If that is true, you have little to expect in that quarter," and Reginald pointed upward, "when your trial comes on, you may find, perhaps, *then*, that the money you have saved and the reputation you have gained are not quite so highly valued *there* as they are at Appleton."

He had walked into the passage while he was speaking, and Jacob Withers turned in the direction of his drawing room, where were assembled some few friends and one young lady, who sung and played superbly. Jacob Withers had one soft place; he liked music, though he did not understand it the least.

"Tom," said he, "show that person out."

Tom sprung forwards, and held the door wide for Reginald, who passed out gloomily and without turning his head.

*   *   *   *   *

The Pennypots sat round the supper table, in the comfortable parlour at the back of the shop. There was lobster and meat pie, and bottled ale. The Pennypots had guests. One was Mrs. Pennypot's sister Anna, who was thirty-two, and unmarried, because, though pretty, she had always been too proud, and too much afraid that her suitors came after her two thousand pounds fortune. The other was a young gentleman from Kent, whose father was a farmer, and who was himself an idler, and was supposed to entertain serious matrimonial intentions towards Miss Anna Tossup and her two thousand pounds.

Mrs. Pennypot was a very, very shrewd woman, an awfully clever woman, a marvel of a housekeeper, and with a never failing flow of sarcasm, which ebbed out in all quarters. She spoke sarcasm, she looked sarcasm; it hid in the corners of her eyes, and lurked at the corners of her lips. She was about thirty-six, pale, rather stout, fond of a rich silk dress and a rich gold chain when she went out; fond of her husband, fond of her children, but fonder than all of "pelf," of the battered pence and crooked sixpences that found their way

into Pennypot's till.   The surly apprentice,
with the irruptive complexion, hated her
mortally, as did also the servants.   So now
you see Mrs. Pennypot as she appeared
to me in the days when I knew her, knew
more of her than was agreeable, in fact.

" To-morrow this dreadful man's trial
comes on," lisped Miss Anna, who wore
little curls, had a fair complexion, and set
up for an excessively refined person.   " It
quite upsets my nerves to hear it talked
of."

Whereupon, they all begun to talk about
it very comfortably.

Mr. Pennypot, of the bald head, and
the large nose, and the bland voice, began
to enter into the minutia of the facts of the
case.

" The points in favour of Withers are
these," said Mr. Pennypot.   " First, there
being no evidence whatever to shew that
he ever had a sack in his possession.
Next, the state of his instruments, which
did not appear more soiled than would

have occurred from the ordinary practice of a surgeon. Lastly, the absence of blood on his own clothes, and on the dissevered limbs of the corpse."

Mr. Pennypot took up a fork, and tapped three of his fingers, one after the other, as he demonstrated these three points.

"Oh, pray hush," said Miss Anna, hiding her face in her hands. "It's dreadful."

"There was motive for the crime, you see," observed the young gentleman from Kent.

"There is generally a motive at the root of people's actions," said Mrs. Pennypot, with a sarcastic smile, and the young gentleman from Kent winced. He was just helping Miss Patty to some pie.

"The case bears very strongly against Withers," said Mr. Pennypot, attacking a claw of the lobster.

"My dear," to Mrs. Pennypot, "have you some hot water?"

"All right," said Mrs. Pennypot. "It will come up presently."

"It bears very strongly against Withers," continued Mr. Pennypot, (when his mind was easy on the subject of the hot water). "His threats, his being on the mountains all night, his spite to Mr. Roggmoore, his being a surgeon, and the plain proof that a surgeon alone had operated upon the body. The questions are, 'What has become of Mr. Roggmoore's clothes? and how did the death occur?' By strangling, I should say. Withers is a tremendously powerful fellow."

"Ill thank you for a little more pie, Mr. Edwards," said Mrs. Pennypot, with a cold smile, then, before she began to eat, she observed, "it is, without exception, the most thrilling, horrible case I ever heard of. Worse than Palmer."

"Oh, yes. Pray don't talk about it any more," pleaded Miss Anna. "I wonder if he will be hung?"

"Figly, in the Borough, is going there with me to-morrow," said Mr. Pennypot, "and, no doubt, it will be the most exciting trial that has been held in London for years."

Just then the hot water came up. Some brandy and water was mixed, and the little party waxed yet more sociable.

*　　　*　　　*　　　*　　　*

CENTRAL CRIMINAL COURT.—Crowds, crowds, crowds, pressing and stifling, and crushing, and quarrelling. Men and women pouring in—some fainting, and having to be carried out; others panting with excitement and eagerness, climbing upon one another's shoulders, "standing upon nothing," to get a glimpse at the barristers and the wigged and ermined judge, and the sharp, chattering solicitors, who were all busy, all apparently treating the momentous affair of life and death which was pending, quite in the way of business— an exciting, pleasurable business, too, it seemed. Ladies in the gallery, ladies with feathers and velvets, who plied fans and put their delicate noses to their scent-cases, and looked down at the court and wondered when the prisoner would be put to the bar.

Now. Yes, there he comes; there he is; there's Withers. A slight hiss greeted his approach.

The clerk of the court called to order, and then Paul was placed in the dock.

The charge was read, and the prisoner was asked to plead guilty or not guilty.

"Not guilty," said Paul, in a clear, distinct voice.

The crowd who were crushing, and stamping, and panting, and standing upon nothing to get a glimpse of him; the ladies who were fanning themselves, and putting their noses to the scent-cases; the Figleys and Pennypots, who occupied good seats near the judge, all fixed their eyes and their attention on Paul.

" How did he look ?"

Oh, reader! six months in gaol; six months of terrible anxiety, of shame, of hopelessness, of exclusion from the fresh air of heaven; six months of frightful days, and burning, fevered nights; six months with a scaffold before his eyes, with the anguish of his mother about his heart, with the bitter consciousness that many who had been his acquaintances and friends believed him guilty; six months of this torture has changed Paul. The colour has gone from his cheek. His eye is bright and keen; but it is the brightness of feverish excitement. He is dressed in a suit of grey; his brown hair is arranged beautifully on his open brow, the purity of his complexion; and the absence of hair on his face give him a youthful, almost a boyish, look. His stalwart form is, however, gaunt and worn. Paul is ill.

"He looks innocent," whispered the ladies in the gallery.

"Young to begin murdering," remarks Figley to Pennypot.

"Bless me," observes that worthy, "I've certainly seen that young man before somewhere, and my impression is not favour able," and he begins to cudgel his brains to find out when and where his mild, respectable eyes have rested on Paul before.

"Silence in the court." The pushing, and stamping, and whispering is hushed.

Mr. Blackett is standing up. He begins for the prosecution. He informs the jury that in the first place the circumstances of this case are already so well known to the public generally, that a recapitulation of the facts would be very wearisome.

"Mothers have pressed their children closer," he alleges, "when the name of the prisoner has been mentioned. At every English hearth-stone his name is execrated. Not an Englishman, with a man's heart in him, but blushes to own him for a countryman." Then the learned gentleman, notwithstanding his asseveration that a repetition of the facts of the case would be wearisome, proceeds to enter minutely into every detail, and to throw the darkest construction upon every word or deed of Paul's which had come to his knowledge.

He goes over again and again those wild threats which the prisoner hurled at the murdered gentleman; he dwells upon his refusal to spend the night at Bïthol; he admits that there was not much cunning shewn in the stowing away of the body. The object appears to have been rather to obliterate the likeness, and destroy the proofs of identity, than to conceal the corpse. He tells the court that the body exactly corresponds in size with that of Mr. Roggmoore, and that though that gentleman had no particular mark about him by which he might have been recognised, yet that his brother, who had been shewn the mutilated limbs of the deceased, had given it as his opinion, though reluctantly, that it was the body of his late brother. He should call witnesses to prove all that he had stated, and he felt convinced that every sensible man must be satisfied in his own mind that the prisoner at the bar was a double dyed villain and bloodstained murderer of the worst stamp. (Hear, hear, from some of the audience.)

Then the learned gentleman sat down, and wiped his brow, and the witnesses for the prosecution were called and sworn in.

" James Timmins, butler to Cecil Percy, Esq., of Percy Priory."

Mr. Blackett rose, and questioned him.

Mr. Timmins gave his evidence with much apparent satisfaction. " Had rushed into the dining parlour on hearing the heavy fall of Mr. Roggmoore; had raised him from the floor, insensible, and bathed in blood ; had distinctly heard the prisoner threaten to have the life of Mr. Roggmoore; had mentioned the mountain road, he believed, as the place where he intended to attack Mr. Roggmoore ; had thrust the prisoner from the door with his own hands."

Cry of " Not likely, judging by your size, and his," from the audience.

Poor Paul looked up, and smiled faintly, at this brag of the little butler's. He had recognised the voice of his former friend,

Gunn, in that sentence, but there was one face wanting which Paul had reckoned on seeing, one face which had never looked at him, save with a true friend's eyes. Reginald Wylde was absent from the court—Reginald, who had promised to stand by him till the last, and Paul sighed bitterly, and looked down.

Mr. Ferret, who was a very sharp-nosed gentleman, begged to be allowed to ask a few questions, and he began to turn Mr. Timmins inside out, metaphorically speaking.

Cross-examined by Mr. Ferret.—" Had lived with Mr. Percy two years. Had not left his last place in consequence of having been discovered listening at the library door when his master was conferring with a gentleman on business. Was not familiarly known among his fellow servants by the name of 'the father,' by which term was meant to be conveyed the fact that Mr. Timmins bore a striking resemblance, in some points, to the individual familiarly known as 'the father of lies.'"

Other witnesses were called.

Madame Williams gave her evidence calmly, and without looking at the prisoner.

Doctor Milton, the valet, and groom of Mr. Roggmoore, who had first discovered the body, all said their say, and were twisted and turned about by Messrs. Ferret and Blackette, alternately for and against.

It began to tell terribly against Paul. He grew sick at heart. Not one eye in all that court seemed moistened with pity for him.

The evidence of the medical gentlemen who had examined the body was very wearisome and lengthy, and wholly incomprehensible to those who were not in the profession.

At last, Mr. Ferret arose and addressed the jury. He stated that though the evidence bore very strongly against the prisoner, he would presently prove that it was impossible for the said prisoner to have obtained the sack in which the body was stowed without the fact transpiring, and that there was not the slightest evidence to shew how death had been caused, or that he, the prisoner, had bought, borrowed, stolen, or had in his possession, at any time, a sack like the one produced in court. It had been contested that the fact of there being no blood either about the prisoner, or the mangled body, went to prove nothing, but he, the learned counsel, was of opinion that it proved much. A man of Withers's impetuous nature would, had he committed murder at all, have done so by quick means, such as stabbing, and would not, as his learned friend Blackett surmised, have first strangled his victim, and then cut up his body. His disposition did not appear to be of that patient or cunning sort." He said a great deal more, and wound up by a touching appeal to the jury on behalf of the prisoner's youth, and a reminder that "up till the time when he was accused of this deed, he had always borne the highest character for integrity and honour."

Then came the summing up, which the learned judge made to bear pretty strongly against Paul, and then the jury retired.

Paul buried his face in his hands. He felt sick unto death. He was expecting the return, the utterance of the fatal word. He was praying that a death without violence might release him from his impending fate, when, suddenly, the whole court began swaying to and fro, and a murmur, like the breaking of the waves on the shore, or the howling of the wind amid the forest trees, was borne to his ears. Then came a breathless pause, and, afterwards, a loud, prolonged, maddened shout, which deepened into a roar; one moment, and Reginald Wylde, with his head uncovered, splashed with the weather, with torn garments, and eyes wild with excitement, made his way to the dock.

There was a tall, fair young gentleman

with him, with a look of great delicacy in his aristocratic face. There was another youth, some five years younger.

Paul recognised Charles and Albert Roggmoore. Several among the audience recognised him also. The whole court was in an uproar, and then Paul knew nothing more, for he sunk fainting on the ground.

*   *   *   *   *

CHAPTER IX.

THE TORN SHEET.

WITH everybody shaking his hands that could get hold of them, with shouts and huzzahs in his ears, with a confused notion that he was somebody else and not himself, and that the whole creation generally had gone mad, Paul was conscious of being almost carried out of court into the streets, where an enormous sea of heads were shouting, and vociferating, and gesticulating. Pale and weak from the effects of his swoon, he was only too glad to be assisted to a cab, into which there presently

followed him Reginald Wylde and Albert
Roggmoore, the latter was beside himself.
He cried and laughed together, and flung
his cap full of silver among the crowd.

"Paul, Paul, I always knew you were
innocent; I always said so; but when I
saw my mother's sorrow and heard her cry,
and when I firmly believed poor Charlie
had been cut up by somebody, 'it was
enough to make a fellow wild. You forgive me, Paul, that I never came near you
in prison. My mother extracted a promise
from me."

Paul shook his proffered hand; but then
he turned to Reginald and grasped *his*
hand in both his own, and looked into his
eyes with the affection of a brother.

Something there was in his friend's face
which startled him—it was full of meaning,
that seemed made up of mingled joy and
horror. His hazel eyes were positively
wild, and, though bright with the tears of
rapture which Paul's deliverance afforded
him, there was yet a certain startled ex-

pression which it seemed to require his utmost nerve and self possession to subdue and to conceal.

"There now," said he at length, when the cab came to a halt before a respectable, quiet, west end hotel, "let us get out here and order a private room. I must get some rest. I have not slept for three nights."

And then they all went into a private room and had dinner, and some good wine; and then they all smoked in silence for an hour.

Paul did not ask one question, his mind was too much agitated to care just then how his deliverance had been effected. He was assured by Reginald that his mother knew of his safety, and that satisfied him.

Afterwards he said he must test his liberty by strolling out.

It was twilight now.

Reginald slept heavily in the arm chair, still in his travel-soiled garments, his head thrown back, his auburn hair tossed wildly about. He had scarcely spoken a word since he had entered the room.

Paul went up to him and placed a soft cushion at the back of his head. Then he left him alone, and, leaning on Albert's arm, he sallied forth into the busy, life-teeming street.

"Where has your brother been all this while?" Paul asked for the first time, when he and Albert found themselves in the vicinity of Leicester Square.

"Ill. Have you not heard?"

"How should I?"

"Ill. Insensible, in some ignorant person's house who knew nothing of his name."

"Impossible! Where has he been ill?"

"Why, in Wales."

"At Bïthol!" exclaimed Paul, coming to a dead halt. "At Bïthol, and that woman is an incarnate fiend."

"What do you mean, Paul? Are you mad?"

"Where did you meet Reginald and your brother?" said Paul, disregarding the other's question.

"In the street, just outside the court," said Albert.

Then Paul became impatient to return to the hotel, and on its threshold Albert left him.

He found Reginald still sleeping. He rang for lights and coffee, and the entrance of these awakened Reginald. He staggered to his feet and turned his face, haggard with excitement, upon Paul.

"Paul, you are saved, my boy!" cried he.

Paul grasped the proffered hand.

"Paul, you are saved, and I am the rightful owner of Percy Priory. Margaret Percy is my first cousin, and Cecil Percy is a bastard."

"What!" shouted Paul, while amaze

held him motionless, and a noise like the booming of the sea was in his ears.

"I am Reginald Percy," said his companion, laying hold of Paul's arm and looking into his eyes. My name, my parentage I could have proved long ago; but here is the unimpeachable proof of Cecil Percy's bastardy," and he drew from his waistcoat pocket a torn sheet of vellum, and held it behind the candle, and the faded characters were distinctly legible.

It was the jagged, half cut, half torn away leaf of a vestry book, a parish register, and this was what was written on it—

Cecil, son of Henry Percy, and Clotilde, Countess St. Autin, baptized the 7th of April, one thousand seven hundred and ninety, in the parish church of Wick, county Northumberland.

AMBROSE LAYTON,
Curate.

John Onwick, Clerk.

"And now, Paul, look here," and Reginald shewed him the certificate of the marriage of Henry Percy and Clotilde, Countess St. Autin, in the parish church at Newcastle, dated December, 1791, the copy of which he had for years kept in his possession.

Paul stood silent with surprise.

"And how did you get this?" he asked, at last.

"It is a long tale. But sit down, and let me tell it to you while we sip our coffee :—

"Towards the close of the last century, that is to say, about seventy years ago, the estates of the Percies consisted of Cheviot Hall, in Northumberland, Croony Park, in Nottinghamshire, and Percy Priory, in Craigshire, Wales. These estates are now in possession of Cecil Percy, and his income is nearly a hundred thousand per annum. Well, in the year 1784, just when the French people were cutting off the heads of their nobles, Henry Percy, the then heir to all these family honours, went over to Paris. He appears to have been a young man of feeling, with poetic fancy and warm heart. It was just at the time when enthu-

, siasm for liberty was at its height. Henry Percy had been bred an aristocrat. All his sympathies were for his own class. In his eyes the republicans were monsters of iniquity, and the nobles suffering martyrs.

"Paul, I often try to realize to myself the nobleman of the courtly old régime, elegant, handsome; standing uncomplainingly, unflinchingly, in the tumbril which conveys him to his death; scorning, with a patient, courtly scorn, the rude insults of the mob; going on to eternity; still the polished Comte, or Vicomte, as it may be, with too much contempt at his heart for the base *canaille* to condescend to fear them even for a moment.

"Once, Henry Percy, who was standing in the crowd, saw going thus to death a young scented noble, with fair hair and fair cheek, and graceful form, with a smile on his slender lip, and his hand placed negligently inside his embroidered waistcoat. Not a gleam of passion in his blue eye, no whiteness even about his handsome mou'

He was going to die as became a de Hadeln and a noble. There was some inexpressible attraction to Henry Percy in the fine face of this young gentleman. He wished to save him. He was a perfect master of the French tongue, and he could at times command a flow of eloquence. He turned round to the crowd, and began to attempt to excite their sympathies in favour of the doomed aristocrat. In vain, in vain. The de Hadelns were a race detested by the people; and Henry learnt that the next day was to witness the execution of a most lovely sister of the Vicomte, a certain Countess St. Auton, who was to suffer by the guillotine.

"Henry saw the handsome young man hewn down by these human butchers, and then he made an inward vow that he would save this lovely Countess St. Auton or die himself. He loved her without seeing her, if that be possible—by which I would convey to you, that fired, excited with rage and pity, and enthusiasm, he felt his whole heart occupied with the as yet unseen Clotilde St. Auton.

"Well, he rescued her. By dint of bribery, and disguising himself, he effected a deliverance; and the sequel was, that the Countess escaped with him to England.

"He must have adored this fair creature in a perfectly poetic, romantic manner. He did not introduce her to his father for a very sufficient reason. The Comte St. Auton, her husband, was alive and fighting in Austria. He was a middle-aged man, and he believed that his wife was dead. She did not apprise him of the fact of her existence. She was a guilty woman. She had been married without her own consent, and without caring for her husband. She lived with Henry Percy, under a feigned name, in a Northumberland village, and Cecil Percy is the offspring of that liaison.

"You see, he has noble blood on both sides. Albeit, he is a bastard; and he takes his stern blue eyes, and self-possessed pride, from his French mother.

"When the news reached Henry Percy of the death of the Count St. Auton he lost no time in marrying the lady whom he had been residing with; but, you see, Cecil was then a twelvemonth old, and his birth had been registered in the manner you have seen.

"Well, it was pretty well known, I suppose, in the obscure village, that the young gentleman and lady were people of rank. They were not married, you will observe, in this village of Wick where their son was baptized, but at Newcastle; and a little while after that Henry made his marriage public, and introduced his fair, French bride to his parents. He did not attempt to conceal the birth of his son. It seemed to be agreed on between them all that the next child was to inherit the estates; and, I suppose, they purposed making a suitable provision for the eldest.

"I do not know how it was that the parents received so kindly a woman who had misconducted herself as this person seems to have done. I can only suppose that morality was laxer seventy years ago than it is now, and that, 'touched,' as Goldsmith's History says, when speaking of Mary Queen of Scots, (if I misquote, set me right), 'touched by her youth, beauty, and misfortunes,' they overlooked her frailty and received her as a daughter.

"She had two other sons, Charles, my father, you will observe, and Roland, much younger than either of his brothers.

The grandparents died, and the boys grew up to manhood. Cecil was the handsomest, Cecil was the tallest, Cecil was the proudest, and he had blue eyes, and an aquiline nose, and a haughty mien; while Charles was short, and broad, and ruddy, with thick lips, a blunt nose, and no pride whatever. He was my father.

"The sons knew nothing of the mystery of their birth. Cecil grew up, believing himself to be the lord of all. The father had not the courage to tell him until he was laid on his death-bed. Then he called his two sons to him (he died comparatively young), and he told how that Cecil was a bastard and no son; and Cecil fell in a fit at the bedside, and was taken up for dead.

" Charles hastened to assure him on his recovery, and after the death of the father, that he had no wish to cast him from his inheritance. He proposed that they should each take an estate, there being three estates and three sons; but Cecil turned away proudly and went to confer with his mother, whose favourite he was.

" All this time Charles was ensnared and enchained by the charms of a beautiful, designing woman, the daughter (you see, I have plebeian blood in me) of a small stationer at Newcastle. They were married secretly. I was born, but not for three or four years after their marriage; and the proofs of this marriage and my birth are in my possession.

"Cecil Percy knew nothing of all this; but, after the death of my grandfather, my father saw no reason for any further concealment.

"My mother, you have seen her, Paul. The dark-eyed woman at Bïthol is my mother. My mother had married for ambition, for the world; without passion, without affection, without love. At first she had thought it a great thing to entrap a great man's younger son; but when my father confided to her his heirship her excitement and determination knew no bounds. She urged him on to take immediate measures to assert his rights and expel his brother.

"Meanwhile Cecil made a secret journey to Wick, stole the key of the church, entered the vestry, and tore out the sheet with the proof of his illegitimacy.

"Goaded on by his ambitious wife, Charles made a like journey, hoping to obtain a legal copy of the sheet; and on a certain winter night he surprised his brother, who was coming out of the church. They fought, and my father obtained possession of the parchment. Well, he did not wish to disgrace his brother, only to come to terms with him. He did not expose the sheet. He hid it somewhere—*where* he would never even tell to his wife (whose existence was all this time a secret); and the end of it was, that while he held this weapon over his brother's head; while he hesitated on the one hand to usurp his family honours, and on the other hand (to please his wife) promised faithfully one day to do so. While Cecil trembled at him, and my mother made him tremble at her in his turn, Charles Percy met with his death in hunting near the Pant-y-dwr, and his secret went down with him to his grave. At last Cecil now had deliverance. He went on in his pride and pomp, for Roland, the youngest son, was innocent of all this affair.

"And now my mother, to whom my father had left a small property, set to

work to find the hidden parchment all in
vain. She bribed the servants, she watched,
she schemed, she waited.

"Cecil Percy, on his part, doubtless, left
no cranny unexplored where by any chance
the torn sheet might have been concealed.
To find it and burn it was his desire. To
find it and claim the estates for me was my
mother's.

"Meanwhile the parchment lay safely
stowed away for eight and thirty years,
under a carved figure of St. Peter on an
oak cabinet in the portrait gallery. It was
found a few days before you were appre-
hended by Charles Bingham Roggmoore;
and my mother, who had really come to
see him on your sister's behalf, was thunder-
struck by finding it in his hands. Her
husband had once shewn it to her years
ago, and she recognised it again; and now
to get it from him that was the question.
No matter whom she sacrificed; no matter
if your young innocent life had been
brought to a shameful close, and a felon's

grave had received you. No matter. No matter. She wanted the torn sheet, and she would have it.

"Paul, this is my mother. Can you wonder at my dislike to women? Can you marvel at my hardness, my disbelief in all things good, or true, or gentle, or pure?

"Well, it seems that the night you left Bïthol for your memorable, lonely walk, Mr. Roggmoore passed the road above my mother's house. Now listen to the devilry of women.

"Old Sarah waited under the trees until the horse passed by, and then she rushed out suddenly with a black cloak over her vile old head. What had they cared if the man had died. As it was, he was thrown from the horse, which shied violently.

"Only three days ago I made a purposed journey down to Appleton, in St. Clements county, to try and induce your Uncle Jacob to stand half the expenses of your trial. I

met with insult of the most stupid, determined kind from that man. More of that,
Paul, another time.

"Well, I went back to the Apple-tree
Inn, and in the commercial room the impending trial was the subject of conversation, and I heard it incidentally mentioned that last summer you had saved
the daughter of Cecil Percy from drowning.

"Instantly I made up my mind to go to
this uncle of mine and see if he would be
more generous to you than your own uncle.
Remember, he has not the smallest idea of
my existence; and at that time, only
three days ago, mark you, I had not
the smallest notion that I should ever
stand in his way, for my mother's anxiety
about the torn sheet has never extended
itself to me.

"I took the train that night to Severntown, arrived there early the next morning,
mounted the stage, and got into Aberglace
by mid-day. I was, of course, aware that

Cecil Percy's health kept him still at home at Percy Priory."

Paul's heart had been beating very quickly during this recital. His cheek burned hotly now, and he asked, in a hoarse whisper,

"Did you see her ?"

" Who ?"

" Margaret. Miss Percy."

" I ? Why Paul, you don't mean —"

"No, no," interrupted Paul, hurriedly. "Its nothing; but go on. What did she say ? How did she look ? Did she seem to care ?"

" You love this woman," Reginald broke forth, angrily; "this girl who is to marry Roggmoore. Oh, Paul ! all men are fools you among the rest; but I'm sorry to tell you I know nothing of your divinity. I didn't go near the Percies. Now listen while I tell you where I did go to :—

" I hired a trap and drove towards Percy Priory, and on my way I passed Bïthol. I have never been near it before; but I knew it from my mother's description in her letters. I could see the chimneys below in the little wooded gorge, and providence must have directed me to go on and enter it. I had travelled, you will observe, since the evening of the day before. The spirit had so far obtained mastery over the flesh that I had not thought of pausing for food or rest once since I had left Appleton; and now, out on the mountains, nature asserted her rights, as the phrase goes. In plain terms, I felt suddenly quite sick for want, and I made up my mind to go and get something to eat from old Sarah, who was left in charge of the house.

"So, leaving my trap standing in the road, I went down the steep path to the lower road, and came in front of the odd-looking, gloomy den, which my mother had built in a freak, that she might watch the Percies. I raised the brass knocker, and clattered and battered at the door for full five minutes, and not a soul came near. Only those distant echoes, which always seem to reverberate after the noise of a knocker on a hall door has subsided into silence, mocked my ears. At last I made my way round to the back, but I found that a great stone wall surrounded the back premises, and there was only a door in this wall, which I did not see the use of attacking.

" I was in a great rage by this time, for I felt sure that my mother had left some absurd orders with Sarah not to open the door at all, for she had written me word that she never admitted any but useful people into her house. By useful, she conveyed those who had any connection, remote or otherwise, with the Percies. I went back, resolved to break the windows, and I began to pick up pebbles, and pelt them into the parlour through the little dingy diamond-paned lattice.

" This brought old Sarah up in a hurry. She rushed to the parlour window, and begun a torrent of abuse, which I cut short by ordering her peremptorily to let me into the house at once.

"The old thing was always a little afraid of me. She knew me at once, and with a dogged civility she admitted me, and ushered me into the ghostly wicked-looking parlour.

"'Why didn't you open the door,' I asked her, angrily.

"She said, 'Her missus had told her never to open it once while she was away.'

"'Why not?' I asked, and then, without giving her time to answer me, I told her to bring me something to eat, and some ale.

"So she brought me some cold meat, and bread and cheese, and a glass of ale, and, at last, after eating and drinking, I rose like a giant refreshed, and prepared to depart.

"Now I happened to catch old Sarah's bleared eyes, and their expression startled me. She manifested great impatience for my departure, also predicting rain, and talking of the lateness of the hour. I suspected something, I scarcely knew what, and I resolved to search the house from top to bottom before I left.

"'I've never been over this house, Sarah,' I said, 'and now I'll search it all, from top to bottom. I want to see what its like.'

"Of course, I hadn't the remotest conception that I should discover anything bearing in the slightest degree on your fortunes; I only thought that old Sarah had something she did not want me to find out hidden in the house, and that whetted my curiosity.

"The moment I said I'd search it all, she became rampant, like an old ass as she is, with fear.

"'You mustn't go for to do it, Mr. Regy, the missus ul be the blessed death of me, I tell you, Sir.'

"Of course, this only made me more curious. To cut it short, I took a candle and began to stamp about the queer place in my usual rough and ready style. I went into the cold stone kitchen, with its saucepan lids shining against the white-washed wall. I penetrated the back premises; then I mounted the stairs, and went into the best bedroom. I suppose from your description, Paul, the one in which your poor sister died; still nothing met my eye to warrant old Sarah's fears and protestations. I found my mother's room, Sarah's, then a long narrow passage, more like those one, finds in houses abroad than in English homes. I began to pace up this passage. Old Sarah now raised a perfect storm of opposition.

"'Yer mustn't, yer mustn't, upon my blessed soul, Mr. Regy; yer shan't then, go down to that there room.'

"I stopped and smiled, amused at her earnestness.

"'What have you got there, Sarah?'

"'Apples and cheese, upon my blessed honour.'

"'Well, I happen to want some apples just now, upon my blessed honour,' said I, and I ran down the passage and came to a halt before a door at the end. This door was locked. Old Sarah stood by, looking very resolute.

"'Open this door,' said I, giving it a violent kick, 'I want to go in.'

"As I kicked the door I heard something stir inside, and a weak voice said 'Please to come in, I want something to drink.' It was a polished man's voice.

"'Who are you?' I roared out; 'how did you come here?'

"'I'm Mr. Charles Bingham Roggmoore, from the Lodge. I've had an illness through a fall from my horse, months ago it must be, I fancy, but indeed I forget everything.'

Instantly I turned upon old Sarah, and caught a savage gripe of her arm.

"'And you knew, you old devil,' I said 'that an innocent man was suspected of the murder of this gentleman, and you've hidden him here six months. Oh, you old demon!'

"She began to whine, ''Twas missus as

was wanted the parchment from him, and he've been too much hurt in's head to understand what she asked him. She only meant to keep him until he got his senses again, for he couldn't make out nothink. She wouldn't a' let the other chap be 'anged, I don't believe.'

"My reply to this was another violent kick at the door, and an order to old Sarah to bring me the key.

"She said, at first, that she had lost it, but she brought it at last, and then I went into the room where the polished, elegant Charles Roggmoore had lain *perdù* for six months. The room itself was comfortable enough. A good bed, a good fire, a good carpet, a window looking into the enclosed space called a garden, and commanding, besides, a view of the peaks of the mountains.

"Mr. Roggmoore looked exceedingly ill, and I found him much shaken in mind. He did not recognise me at first, but when I made myself known to him as Reginald Wylde, he seemed delighted to see me.

"Having locked old Sarah out, and taken a seat beside him, he began to give me an account of his frightful horse accident. His skull had been terribly fractured, he said, and he had lain perfectly insensible for, he supposed, six weeks or two months. He had been coming from Percy Priory, he told me, in the autumn of the past year, when, at one part of the road, something black had jumped before his horse, which had shied violently, and pitched him upon his head. He had known nothing more until he had found himself in that room, nursed and attended upon by two old women, one rather lady like, the other a monster of ugliness and stupidity. He said that his power of speech had only returned to him within the last few days, and since the absence of the old lady, whom he had supposed was the mistress of the house. He said that he was surprised none of his family had inquired after him, and that he had not seen a doctor; but his apathy, and the little astonishment he manifested, was something sad to contemplate. I suspected foul play on the part of my mother, because Sarah had let fall something about his having found a parchment.

"I asked him plainly if the old lady had questioned him since his senses had returned to him.

"'Yes,' he told me with a puzzled look, 'something about a parchment which he had found under the figure of St. Peter, which was loose in its socket, in the carved cabinet in the portrait gallery at Percy Priory. He had found a parchment there, and secreted it there again before starting on that night when he met with his accident.' His memory had failed him on several points, and though he remembered the finding of the parchment he totally forgot whom it concerned, 'the lady who had so kindly nursed him most probably, for she had certainly made enquiries respecting it more than once lately, when he had been totally unable to respond to her queries.'

"With my natural joy at having within my grasp at last the parchment which was to give me my just inheritance and my name, there mingled a feeling of deep pity for the poor wreck of a man before me, and of fierce abhorrence for my mother's fiendlike conduct. I dreaded leaving the young man alone with the unscrupulous old Sarah, and hastily telling him that I would return in about an hour, I gave him what cooling drink he wanted, and then I went out, and took the precaution to lock him in and put the key in my pocket.

"I then sought old Sarah, and after some severe questioning I extracted the truth from her.

"She admitted that by her mistress's orders she had waited under the trees with a cloak over her head, intending if Mr. Roggmoore passed that way that night to start out and cause him to fall from his horse. They had hardly thought that he would have met with so severe a fracture, merely meaning to break an arm, or inflict a few bruises so as to necessitate nursing, and to give them an opportunity of coaxing the parchment from him; but to their dismay, his fall on the rocky road was nearly proving fatal, and for months it was impossible to extract more than 'Yes,' or 'No,' from him.

"They searched his clothes, but not finding the torn sheet they actually calmly contemplated waiting for his recovery of speech, and I don't think my mother would have said a word to save your life. She would have been afraid of Roggmoore's family taking him from her care, and of so losing her influence over him before obtaining the parchment.

"I got into my trap, and drove to Percy Priory. I got in the back way by a ruse telling the servants that I was commissioned to arrange the pictures differently in the portrait gallery. They gave me a lamp and conducted me to the place, and there they left me. I walked on until I came to the identical little cabinet, and in less than two minutes I had recognised St. Peter on the water, drawn the figure out, and secured the parchment.

I hastened out, and was accosted on the grand staircase by my haughty uncle, who asked me what I did there, I made an excuse, got back to Bithol, and told Roggmoore you were nearly being hanged for the supposed murder, and let me do him the justice to say he was as anxious as myself to get into court in time to stop the proceedings.

"We drove back to Aberglace that night, where we rested a few hours, and he was recognised at the Bull, and the whole town was in an uproar. The eighty miles of stage is the reason that no telegraphic message reached town in time to stop proceedings. After we had had a bath, a change of linen, and a supper, we took post horses on to Severntown. We preferred surprising you in court to sending a telegraphic message from thence. It was evening, you know, before we made our startling *entrée*, and now, Paul, my boy, that's enough news for one night. Let us get to bed. To-morrow you shall ask as many more questions as you please."

CHAPTER X.

QUESTIONS.

PAUL and Reginald sat late over their breakfast the next morning. Paul was full of questions, some of which it puzzled Reginald to answer.

"I remember, when I first went down to Aberglace, the old Doctor gave me a slight sketch of the Percy family. He told me they were an unfortunate family. He mentioned Charles having been killed by a fall from his horse, but it was the youngest son, Ronald, whom he described as having

married a bad, low person, and that Cecil
Percy had pensioned him off, on condition
of his living abroad. He said that this
brother, the wife, and a son, were all
dead. Is that true? Quite true. Cecil
Percy seems to have monopolized all the
pride of the family. My mother, you
know, was the daughter of a stationer,
and Roland's wife, I suppose, was a
thorough bad creature. She is dead and
gone though, as well as her son."

"Whom did Cecil marry? Who was
Margaret's mother?"

"A daughter of Lord Huntley, a Scotch
title. Margaret inherits a fine Scotch estate
in right of her mother."

"And now, Reginald, how is it that
such a noble fellow as you are has such
a vile mother?"

"I am not a noble fellow at all, Paul.
I am a lazy, selfish, good for nothing
hound, with—"

"Reginald," interrupted Paul, "listen to

me for a moment. There are six young women in Aberglace, named Perfectway. They are milliners, you know."

" No, I don't know. How should I ?"

" Well, be quiet a moment, will you? Six young women, named Perfectway, and they are milliners. Well, everybody in the wisely judging town of Aberglace is of opinion that the Miss Perfectways are perfect. No gossip about the Miss Perfectways. Not a bit of it. Although Aberglace is the nicest little town for hashing up wicked little stories that was ever known, it dares not say one tiny unkind thing of the Miss Perfectways. And yet they have beaux, with whom they walk about. These beaux go to tea with them. I've been to tea with them, but never a whisper against the Perfectways. They're never called 'fast' or 'giddy,' or any other of those spiteful little names that are heaped so lavishly on other people in Aberglace."

" Well, there's nothing in that. They are perfect, I suppose. Aren't they ?"

"I'm sure I don't know. I really think they are as good as most other people, but I don't consider them a bit better. I don't think them goddesses at all, only well behaved, tidy little milliners. But Aberglace thinks them faultless, and I want you to guess why."

"How should I guess?"

"Well, I'll tell you. They always praise themselves, Reginald; and short as is my experience of the world, I have come to the conclusion that it always values you at your own estimate. If you keep on crying out, 'I'm a grand fellow,' 'I'm a clever fellow,' the world will soon echo your words, and believe what you say of yourself. Now take a lesson from poor Paul. Don't run yourself down. It's very frank of you to say what you think of yourself. You are not a lazy hound, and as for selfish, Reginald, you don't know what it means."

"Don't begin to praise me, Paul; but if you like I'll tell you a little about my

childhood and my mother.   She was
tolerably fond of me, I think; not over
affectionate, but never cruel.   I remember
living in the North, somewhere near to
Cheviot Hall, with her and old Sarah, when
I used to go to the village school to learn
my alphabet; at that time we were called
Brown.   My Mother was all the time I
suppose trying after the torn sheet.   Once
'she managed to get old Sarah hired there
as charwoman, and once she actually went
there herself as seamstress, and she used
to go poking about in the night and search-
ing every drawer for the parchment.   Afterwards she took into her head to go abroad,
because my father had made several trips
to Paris, Rome, and Vienna, and she
thought he might have stowed it away
in some place or other there.   We lived
abroad for years, and that gave me my
first love for my art; as I grew older I
threw my whole soul into it.   I swore that
I would become a painter.   My mother
neither encouraged me, nor dissuaded me.

I felt my way on unassisted; for my mother herself, her selfish aims, her worldliness, her coldness, her unscrupulous code of principles, I early imbibed a distaste. I flung the thought of the torn sheet to the winds, and I went over to Dublin to graduate, for I wished to have the education of a gentleman. My mother you know has an independent income of four hundred a year. I took the name of Wylde, and ever after I claimed Ireland as my country, for I considered that I had no country and no name. My father had realised the property my mother enjoyed, and it was paid to her in the name of Brown regularly every quarter. I liked Ireland very much. I fell in love there, Paul."

" Did you ?"

" Yes, with an opera dancer—the only woman I ever cared for. I make light of it now, and the old wound is healed; but I assure you it was a deep sorrow to me when I found that my idiol was clay, and worthless clay, too. I came away thinking my whole life was to be a blank; but no, a certain nobleman happening to take a great fancy to one of my paintings, my name rose, I became famous. I found comfort in dinners, and dissipation, and—"

"Hush, hush," cried Paul, "remember the Miss Perfectways. I am sure you only did what was right."

"Exactly so," said Reginald, "I became a model of perfection, which I remain to this day."

CHAPTER XI.

AN UNINTERESTING CHAPTER.

"AND now," said Paul, rising, "I will go to my mother. She must be better and calmer by this morning. And will you come with me, Reginald?"

"Yes, I've never seen your mother, Paul. I suppose she's a better specimen of the genus than my mother."

"Yes, she is affectionate and warm-hearted. But, Reginald, what do you purpose doing with your wonderful torn sheet? Shall you call upon Mr. Percy, or get your solicitor to write to him?"

"Oh, I shall call upon him. I hear he'll be in town this week. If he will come to an understanding without litigation I shall be pleased, but I must get a legal copy of this vestry sheet first at a lawyer's office."

So Paul and Reginald went to an office in Chancery Lane, and had the birth of Cecil Percy duly registered; and then they went to the lodgings in the New Kent Road, near to Horsemonger Lane Jail, where poor Mrs. Withers had fixed her residence. They found her in bed, ill from excitement and joy, which the news of Paul's deliverance had occasioned

There was a tall, slim girl of fourteen in the parlour, with dark eyes like poor Emma's; but they were gentler, and the whole expression of the face was sweeter. This girl embraced Paul warmly when she heard his name. This was little Patty, Paul's sister, come from school to nurse her mother.

Reginald looked at her a great deal,

and told Paul when she had gone out of the room that he should like to paint her portrait.

When Mrs. Withers appeared, she first embraced Paul, then flung herself upon Reginald, and wept and blessed him with Scripture texts, as was her wont, and when Patty came in again they heard what the world said about Charles Bingham Roggmoore's detention.

It was currently reported that he had been thrown from his horse, and his skull fractured, and that the people who had nursed him were too ignorant to know of the circumstances of the case.

Reginald well knew that a report of that kind could not long be believed or substantiated; but he saw that it would give his mother time to escape to the Continent, for, of course, she had made herself amenable to the laws by her suppression of the fact of Mr. Roggmoore's existence; not to speak of the attack made on him when riding, and her being the wilful cause of his terrible accident.

As it was, he, of course, naturally favoured the idea which had got wind, that ignorance, not wilfulness, was the cause of the detention of Mr. Roggmoore.

Felix heard the news of his brother's deliverance. Felix had rejoiced as much as it was possible for him to rejoice at the good fortune of another.

Paul and Reginald spent all that day in the New Kent Road, and towards evenin Felix actually condescended to creep in. He found Reginald, his mother, Paul, and Patty partaking of an early supper of Welsh rabbit, of which Reginald professed himself fond.

Felix put his scented handkerchief to his nose, to counteract the odour of the toasted cheese; he kissed his mother, and then offered his hand to Paul and Reginald. The latter gave him two cold fingers, and three or four colder words.

Paul did not resent his brother's unkindness; he spoke to him civilly, not even coldly; looked with a half smile at the frugal supper board, but did not press him to eat.

"Oh, Paul, my dear fellow, the papers are full of you to-day; the reaction is tremendous, you are praised immensely."

"The praise," said Reginald, coldly, "is quite as worthy of remark as was the abuse."

"Have you heard anything of Mr. Roggmoore?" asked Paul.

"Yes; they say he's almost an idiot; he forgets from one hour to another. I heard Lord Ecart say so to-day in our studio. He is with his mother. They say the Earl, his uncle, died last night, and he has just come into the title when he has lost his brains."

"A loss which it would be impossible for some people to sustain," said Reginald, drily. "I think Mr. Roggmoore *had* brains once. Perhaps, now, if he has lost them he will do as well as some of our acquaintances who never had any to lose."

So Reginald made himself obnoxious to poor Felix, who soon took his hat and left the little family party; and I am quite of opinion that if he had never come back his loss would not have been too severely felt by two of the company.

The next few days was given up to the arranging of Paul's affairs. Doctor Milton sent him his quarter's salary, and all his luggage from Aberglace had to be claimed and taken possession of.

He still remained quietly in the New Kent Road with his mother, while the public excitement in regard to him knew no bounds. *The Times* gave a startling account of his graces and virtues. It did more — it called upon Englishmen to come forward and make amends substantially to the young noble being who had suffered six months of unjust captivity. It dwelt upon his patience, his courage, his wronged Sister, his widowed mother, and then it waited quietly the result of its application. It was an astonishing result; contributions from all sides poured into its office. Noblemen, physicians, surgeons, enthusiastic rich ladies, who were odd, and eccentric, and disagreeable generally, came down with their "dust" in grand style, and before three weeks were over his head, Paul was the actual possessor of the sum of £10,000 sterling. He placed it in the funds, and settled his mother in a pretty cottage at Hammersmith.

Of course all this took time, but I mention these facts here, because as I draw towards the end of my task I am afraid I may leave something untold, and so you understand perfectly I hope, Reader, that Paul is in possession of a nice income of three or four hundred a year, that his mother is provided for, and that the press and the public generally are of opinion that he is all but a demi-god.

The mystery of the body in the sack remains uncleared up to this day; like the Waterloo Bridge sack, and the Road Child Murder, it is still among the hidden things of darkness. It is, however, shrewdly suspected that it was a trick of a body snatcher who had also some surgical skill, and that perhaps had some of the graves in the Aberglace Churchyard been searched, some corpse might have been missing. *The Times* and the local journals are of this opinion, and that it was probably some pauper's body, which the thief intended, if possible, selling to the doctors perhaps at Aberdare, which was the nearest town on the road the man was pursuing. It is conjectured that, suddenly struck with terror, this person had cast his burden where it was found on the mountain; or else that overcome with fatigue, he had found himself unequal to the task he had undertaken. Whoever he was, he was highly culpable that he did not come forward to state what he knew of the case. The supposed identification of the riding gloves with those of Mr. Roggmoore was found to be a fallacy.

That gentleman did not manifest the

least rancour towards Madame Williams, whom he supposed to have been a kind nurse, unconscious of his name and position. He never totally recovered his faculties, and his memory failed him on several points. He was now the Earl Danvers, and to one thing he was constant. He still wished to marry Miss Percy. But it was not long before a cry was raised, and a very active inquiry entered into as to the whereabouts of Madame Williams. She had, however, ere that time escaped to the Continent, where she lived under a feigned name, and defied detection.

It was warmly contested by some legal gentlemen that Paul would never have been hung, even had Mr. Roggmoore's existence not been proved; that there being no proof whatever of his having had a sack in his possession at any time would alone have cleared him, since he had left Bithol perfectly empty handed, and had called nowhere on the way. Be this as it may, one thing is certain, that in that case Paul would only have escaped with a stained name, and that now he had come off " glorious and free."

And now we must go back a little in our narrative, to where Paul is standing on the hearth-rug, in the little sitting room in the New Kent Road, one bright morning, and Reginald is standing by him, urging him to accompany him to the Percies, who are totally ignorant of the power Reginald possesses over them. They are now, he says, at their grand town house in St. James's Square, and Paul naturally feels very shy about intruding himself into their presence.

"But you come as my friend and witness," urged Reginald.

So at last Paul consented. They stepped into a cab, and drove straight to the superb house, and were actually admitted into the august presence of Cecil Percy, who was sipping chocolate by the fire in the library.

"Some business about tenants," he asked, carelessly.

"No," said Reginald, bluntly. "Some business about myself."

Just then Mr. Percy's eye happened to rest on Paul, whose colour was changing, and whose heart was beating with the expectation of seeing Margaret.

"Oh, is it you, Mr. Withers? I'm glad of the result of your misfortunes, take a seat."

Wonderful condescension for Cecil Percy! so Paul took a seat, but Reginald remained standing. He began at once.

"Mr. Percy, I am your nephew, the lawful son of your brother Charles. I can prove my birth any time you like."

Mr. Percy turned a shade whiter, and Paul fearing the effects of Reginald's communication on his frame, went up to him and begged him to be calm.

"I am perfectly calm, thank you," said Mr. Percy, putting Paul aside haughtily; and then turning his white face towards Reginald, he remarked, "Well, Sir, you say you are my nephew—I did not know I had the honour of your relationship."

"It is no honour, and it is no shame," returned Reginald. "I have always, I hope, been an honest man. The name under which I have lived — Reginald Wylde—is not, perhaps, totally unknown to you? I have never done anything, Mr. Percy, to disgrace it."

Mr. Percy started, but regained the mastery over himself immediately.

"What is the purport of your visit, then, Mr. Wylde?" said he, with a scarcely perceptible sneer.

"Only to claim my estates, which you unjustly hold," returned Reginald, who was fired at the other's contempt.

"Unjustly," faltered Mr. Percy, with a last attempt at haughtiness.

"Yes, Sir, I have in my possession the torn sheet which proves your birth before the marriage of your parents."

"Mr. Withers, I feel ill," said Mr. Percy imploringly.

Paul unloosened his cravat, and made him stand upon his feet.

"Lean upon me, Mr. Percy," said Paul, "walk slowly round the room—there, now do you feel better?"

Reginald meanwhile prepared to lay the case before Mr. Percy.

I hate law details so I shall shorten this part of my story, and only tell you the result of the conversation of that morning. Mr. Percy came amicably to terms, and Reginald was as generous as was his nature. Percy Priory, with its unencumbered rent roll of thirty thousand a year, was all he claimed for himself. The great north estates Mr. Percy was to enjoy for his life-time, but in case Reginald married and had a son, they were to descend to that son, at Mr. Percy's death. The little Cecil was to have the Nottinghamshire estate of twenty thousand a year, tied upon him and his heirs for ever, and Mr. Percy, who found that his fraud of long years past was brought home to him became contrite, almost humble. We will not dwell upon his humiliation. He was obliged after all to admit that Reginald was a gentleman and a true Percy at heart.

I don't know how the pale and peerless Margaret bore the news of this loss of property. I know she married Earl Danvers very soon after, and covered her family discomfiture with a very splendid wedding. I suppose she never loved her husband, but her conduct was blameless, and she gave the most splendid balls, and wore the finest diamonds in London, and I hope they made her happy—very likely they did.

CHAPTER XII.

ANOTHER NEW YEAR'S EVE.

MORE than two years have rolled away. Two years! Yes. And what has Paul been doing all the time?—Paul, established in London, with no dread of poverty before him, with his mother and sister provided for, and the world smiling at him generally.

Paul is a prosperous Paul now, upward and onward, he has climbed his way in his profession manfully, and already his brightest aspirations seem nearly being realised.

He is already, though young, beginning to be famous; beginning to carve out a fortune for himself. His boyish notion, that the crowded, stirring city, where men jostle at every turn, was the place for him, appears more true to him than ever.

He is a friend to the poor and the sinners, and to those whose faces shame has covered. The road he is treading, made bright by his goodness and his talents, has still some charms for him.

What of his love? Is it dead? His love for the bright lady who is now a countess, and who has never given him a passing thought? Do such loves ever die out? Cannot most of us remember a time when life seemed valueless? when existence seemed swallowed up in passion? when the heart and the spirit were scorched by a continual fire? And when time, and reason, and circumstance, and nature, have conspired to remove the scalding pain and to teach us wisdom, what then? Shall we be like "dumb driven cattle?" or, like

Paul, shall each of us strive to become a hero in the strife?

Before many years Paul did really become a great doctor, waited on by courtly patients, sought for, valued, beloved.

But now I am going to tell you of a certain New Year's Eve. Have you forgotten that when Paul first met Reginald Wylde, it was on a certain freezing New Year's Eve, on Waterloo Bridge, and the two made a compact that henceforth, every New Year's Eve they were to spend together. And now Paul is staying at Percy Priory, for one week, borrowed from his arduous duties. He arrived only last night, and this night, this New Year's Eve, Reginald has thrown his house open, and is entertaining almost the whole county with a grand ball and supper.

And Paul is as much sought, as much thought of as Reginald himself. He is known to be his chief friend, reported to be his heir, and some of the high and mighty of Aberglace, who are there, smile upon him very sweetly indeed.

This was not the first visit Paul had paid to Percy Priory. He had been there several times before, and Reginald was very intimate with the Hartleys, and Paul and Flora are talking together at the window looking into the lordly park, while the band is discoursing sweet music. The splendid ball room, with its blaze of lights, its happy groups of young and old, the conservatory, with its gorgeous flowers, in ful magnificence; outside, the white, still, spotless snow, covering the woods with its robe of purity; above, the bright, quiet moon. And the young, brave, honest Paul, and the gentle, divine Flora, are looking out upon the white world, and he is pleading, " To stand by me in joy and in sorrow, to halo my whole life by your presence, to be my hope, my love, my wife."

She did not speak, and he went on again.

" Toiling from morning till evening, missing a sweet voice to welcome my returning, looking in vain for a sweet face at my hearthstone. Say, must not my life be joyless? If I might but claim that dear hand as mine, my own."

Flora put it confidingly into his, and her tears of joy fell on it fast and thick. She loved Paul.

Later that evening Paul went into the conservatory, and came suddenly upon a couple. One was Reginald, the other was a pretty dark-eyed girl we have seen once before, and Reginald held her hand in his own, and whispered love in her ear, and at first Paul felt hot and angry when he recognised his sister, but Reginald burst into a joyous ringing laugh.

"Don't knock me down, Paul. Little Patty has promised to be my wife. Let me present you to Mrs. Reginald Percy."

We may hint here that Cecil Percy the younger never came in for the great North Estates.

CHAPTER XIII.

ABOUT A NAMELESS ONE.

AND what became of Emma's child? That child, who, in the emphatic language of village gossips, "Never oughtent to have been born." "Poor hapless one," whom all felt it to be a duty to provide for, but from which duty all shrunk timidly. And yet the boy was housed, and fed, and sheltered, and, as he grew older, he was taught, and sent to school, and even welcomed home again in his holidays, with something like affection. *Something like affection*, but not the genuine, gushing, fond, foolish tenderness which a happier birth would have in-sured him. He lived with his grandmother, and she was kind to him, but the remem-brance of his fair dead mother, and his proud, false father, stood like a thick cloud between her and the boy.

When Paul saw him, his brow would knit itself into a frown, and he would some-times look away from the little face, which brought so keenly to his mind the darkest chapter in his life's history.

The child was an old-fashioned, weird creature, with Emma's eyes, large, fierce, black as night, and with, sometimes, the weary old look in them, that look her mo-ther remembered so well. And then the boy inherited her fiery, indomitable spirit; her passionate nature, her fits of sullenness. His friends trembled for his future. He was never beaten. Nobody liked to lay a finger upon the forlorn one, except in kindness. But, still, many shook their heads, and observed, in low tones, that John (they had given him this plain baptismal name), was a difficult child to deal with. He often asked strange questions about his parents, and, before long, the gossip of servants unfolded to his young mind the story of his birth, and his wrongs distorted and mangled into even greater hideousness than the naked truth itself possessed, frightful as was that story and its accompaniments, and at seven years old, John sat silent and stern in a corner of his chamber, refusing to stir, to eat any food, turning away alike from scold_ ing and from threats.

"Now, master John, come and eat your dinner like a good boy," said his nurse. But master John only set his teeth hard, and glared at his nurse like a small savage. He would not even answer her.

Then his grandmother was called, and she was told how that master John wouldn't eat, or speak, or move, all along of what that good-for-nothing girl, the housemaid, had told him.

"It was you," burst forth the boy, fiercely. "You said my father was alive,

and wouldn't own me; and you said my
mother was a bad one. That's just what
you said. And that everybody was sorry
I hadn't died, granny and all. And, oh,
I wish I was dead, I do, I do, I do," and,
blind with fury, the poor child rolled on
the floor, and bit his own hands until they
bled.

The nurse whined, and denied, and
wept, and was dismissed forthwith, and
the child was coaxed, and some attempt
was made to fondle him by his grandmother, but she did it nervously, and the
boy shook her off angrily, crying out, "Get
away, get away granny. You know you
want me dead and cold in a coffin, boxed
up, and nailed down, like the boy that
died next door."

In the midst of this affray, Paul and his
wife arrived to call upon Mrs. Withers, and
they were entreated to come upstairs and
try to soften the little fury.

"Come, my boy, what's all this about?"
said the kind frank voice of Paul—Paul

who had been married four years, and had two lovely boys of his own. "What's all this about?" said Paul.

"About me, about my mother, and I wish I was dead, and I hate you, uncle Paul," said the boy. "If I was big enough I'd fight you, I would."

"Why?"

"Because you think"—a convulsive sob —"its a pity I"—a sob again—"didn't die when my mother did."

Now Paul was really guilty of having at one time given utterance to that sentiment, and he coloured deeply, and cleared his voice, but, before he could speak, his wife drew him gently aside, and urged some suit with great earnestness.

"Older than our boys," said Flora, "need never be jealous of them. A child who must be led by love and kindness. Remember, Paul, your dead sister's own child. And she thought she was a wedded wife. Believed it, Paul, as firmly as I believe that I am yours."

"But such a temper, dearest. He will kill our meek youngsters at home."

"Oh, no, Paul. They will look up to him. He is a clever child. He only wants management. I can make him love me I know."

Not to spin out a tale, I must say, hastily, that Paul and Flora succeeded in persuading Mrs. Withers to part with John, and John became domiciled in Russell Square, with Paul's boys.

He soon loved Flora with all the warmth of which his nature was capable; he softened and improved under her gentle rule, and he manifested great talent, great aptitude to learn. In the genial atmosphere of love which pervaded Paul's household, the little ill-conditioned plant began to put forth sweet flowers, and it might have ripened into a tree of goodly growth, but Heaven willed otherwise.   *   *   *

Fifteen years have passed away since the marriage of Charles Bingham, Earl Danvers, to Miss Percy—five years more than

the time she had herself stated was sufficient to make the warmest love subside
into indifference.

How is it then with the Lady Danvers,
she who has never loved at all?

It is early spring, and the Earl and his
wife are staying at their estate in Cumber-
land, one which the present owner inherits
from his late uncle.

The Earl is in feeble health, his valet has
wheeled him out to the terrace in front of
the breakfast room windows, and he is
looking wistfully on the prospect. Tiers
on tiers of blue distant mountains—the
summits of some of them lost in gold
coloured mist; Ullswater glancing like a
liquid sheet of silver; and the richly
wooded plain stretching from the mountain's feet to the verge of the park which
owns him master.

He was very rich; he was but in the
prime of life; friends and flatterers fawned
upon him; but ill health had set its seal
upon him. Already the brightly-painted

apples of promise and pleasure were turned to ashes in his mouth, and the once careless man of the world found himself at one and forty childless and almost hopeless.

Both of his brothers had died of fever within two days of each other.

The peerless Margaret had brought him no children.

And now, was he to go down to his grave, and leave no heir to his title and honours? Was his name to die out for ever?

Long and wistfully the sick man gazed at the ridges of blue mountains, now darkened in shadow, now dazzling in the sunshine. Did they recall another mountain land, and a white house amid whispering foliage, and a bright-haired girl who had loved him until death? and that Dull Stone House?—that frightful fall?—his wife? Yes, Emma *had* been his wife in the sight of God. He sometimes thought of the unseen now. Most of us do at whose feet graves have opened, hiding from us those of our households with whom we have been familiar as with our own lives.

Two dead faces in narrow boxes; two voices hushed for ever; two brothers gone from among men.

He might linger long, or he might die within the year. The unseen, the unknown, the irrevocable past; the wronged dead, the wronged *living*.

What if the birth of that son could be rendered honourable? Could any legal process effect it? The priest had blessed his union with Emma, and he had deceived the priest in pretending to be of the Catholic faith. Could he own himself in the wrong and claim the son whom he knew to have been adopted by Paul the surgeon? At least he would consult his wife. And he was wheeled back into the breakfast room, and there, by the brightly burning fire, he awaited the coming of Lady Danvers, whom he sent to summon.

She came in, fashionably dressed; stout and matronly; handsome still; a little, just

a little, more energy in her manner than of
yore.

She did not look wearied and disappointed as one might have fancied. The
rank, and the grandeur, and the diamonds,
and the fashion had filled her life to the
brim. She had nothing left to wish for.
She did not love children.

"Margaret, I shall not live long, and
when I die there is no one to take my title
and my lands."

"I thought there was some cousin?"

"No, Margaret, not one."

"It is very odd," said Margaret carelessly, "but you are not going to die yet
you know."

"How do I know? But even if I live
I shall never have an heir."

Margaret looked at the fire, and said,
"What is the use of vexing?"

"I am not vexing, Margaret, but I have
a thing to propose to you. What if I seek
out the son I have by my first marriage?"

"Marriage," echoed Lady Danvers.

"It was a sort of marriage. Perhaps money and interest might suffice to establish the legitimacy of that boy."

"What a frightful humiliation," said Margaret, clasping her white hands. "Would that we had a son."

"But we have not," said the Earl, sadly, "there is the rub. This boy has been adopted by the surgeon. I intend to seek him out."

"He will be horribly vulgar," said Margaret, shuddering.

"That may soon be rectified. Remember it is an heir I seek."

"Have your own way," said Margaret, coldly.

And so it was settled that the nameless one was to be sought after, with intent to make him the heir to the titles and lands of Danvers.

CHAPTER XIV.

CLAIMED.

" There has been a frightful accident," said a cabman, in the blocked up crossing in the Regent's Circus. " That is what the crowd is about."

It was Earl Danvers' coachman he addressed, which said coachman could make no way at all against the enormous crowd of vehicles and pedestrians. The wheels of his lordship's carriage were pressed closely against the wheels of another conveyance, an omnibus. Lord Danvers put his head out of the window.

"What is the matter?"

"An accident, my lord."

"What is it?"

"What is it?" said the coachman to a man in the crowd.

"A house burnt down. A fire. Six people killed. An old woman burnt, two young men crushed."

These scraps of information were conveyed to Lord Danvers. He leaned back in his carriage, and presently there was way made for his lordship's passage, and he drove on into Russell Square, and stopped at the door of Paul's house, and when his name and title was announced he was admitted, and shewn into a large handsome room on the first floor, and presently Paul Withers and Charles Bingham Roggmoore, Earl of Danvers, stood alone in each others presence, as they had stood last, more than fifteen years ago, at Percy Priory.

The two men would hardly have recognised each other. The feeble earl, with hair streaked with grey, bore no resem-

blance to the polished, calm, insolent Roggmoore of long ago, and Paul was a grave,
thoughtful man, with a pale cheek, and a
brow on which time had already "written
wrinkles."

He bowed gravely to the earl, and the
earl returned the salute quietly, almost
humbly. Paul Withers had last stood
before him as the frantic avenger of the
sins of his youth. Now he did not even
look reproachfully at him, only with a sort
of mild surprise.

"Mr. Withers," began the earl, "you
have adopted the, your, in fact, my son,
have you not?"

"Yes, my lord."

"Will you give him up? I wish to
claim him, and I find I can have his birth
legitimatized. In fact, I have no heirs,
and so—"

"And so," said Paul, quietly, "You
wish to reclaim him. I will consult John."

"I do not fear the result of your con-
sultation," said the earl. "And have you
named him John?"

"Yes," returned Paul.

At this moment there came a crowd in front of the windows, and the tread of many feet, and the sound of many voices, and the crowd stopped in front of Paul's house, and then the knocker was raised, and a heavy blow was hammered ominously against the door.

"An accident," said Paul, calmly, when he saw a cab stop. "Your lordship will excuse me a moment," and he went into the passage, and met *something* borne upon mens' shoulders, *something* from which had passed that living soul which is the breath of God, and only the mortal part remained, "the shuffled off coil" of the immortal. It was the dead face of a handsome youth of fifteen or sixteen! The whiteness of the calm features showed that death had happened by drowning, as well as the dripping clothes and hair.

Paul uttered an exclamation of agony. The child of Emma was stretched dead before him.

How had it happened? The details of the story were horribly commonplace, perhaps Lady Danvers would have said.

The dead youth had plunged into the Serpentine to save a butcher's lad who was drowning—a mere plebeian, of whom he knew nothing—and both had perished;— the young errand lad and the nameless son of a noble. Papers in his pocket had identified his residence, and here he was, stretched lifeless at the feet of the betrayer of his mother, just when that betrayer had come to seek him eagerly, with wealth and honours to tempt him to his arms.

It needed only for Paul to point sobbing to the corpse, to overwhelm the Earl with the consciousness of his loss. And then Paul spoke.

"Sixteen years ago so lay dead and still and oblivious of all things Emma, his mother. My lord, my lord, it is the will of God: life has been extinct for hours. You have no son."

And then the Earl Danvers bent his

head in lowliness, and while his tears mingled with those of Paul, he owned his sin
and the justice of God with true humility,
perhaps, for the first time; and the nameless
one found a rest doubtless in the better
land, and was mourned on earth by loving
hearts, while the Earl of Danvers went
childless to his tomb, and his lands and
titles became the inheritance of a stranger.

15 JY 62

THE END.

PRESERVATION SERVICE

SHELFMARK 1.26.24..b.7

THIS BOOK HAS BEEN
MICROFILMED (20 06   )
                    N.S.T.C.

MICROFILM NO *SEE RPM*

Lightning Source UK Ltd.
Milton Keynes UK
UKHW050649131122
412129UK00004B/15